Air
Band
Radio
Guide

FOURTH EDITION

Graham Duke

D1425999

Ian Allan
PUBLISHING

Acknowlegements

My grateful thanks are due to the many organisations, and individual persons, who have helped with the preparation of this publication. Although it is not possible to mention everyone, special thanks are acknowledged to the following:

Aerad, London; Civil Aviation Authority, London (Public Relations Department); Flightdeck (The Aviation Shop); Garex Electronics; Javiation; Jeppesen, Frankfurt; Lowe Electronics; National Air Traffic Services (NATS) — London ATCC; NATS — Scottish and Oceanic; NATS — Frequency Management Division; Nevada; Radiocommunications Agency, London; Radio Research, Stoke-on-Trent; Royal Air Force, No 1 AIDU, Northolt; Sandpiper Communications; Servisair, Bramhall, Cheshire; Shannon Aeradio, Ireland; Steepletone, Waters & Stanton.

Finally, my special thanks to Enid and Jane for their assistance with the preparation of the manuscript.

Contents

First published 1992
Reprinted 1993
Second edition 1995
Reprinted 1996
Third edition 1997
Fourth edition 1999

ISBN 0 7110 2647 5

Published by Ian Allan Publishing

an imprint of Ian Allan Publishing Ltd, Terminal House, Shepperton, Surrey TW17 8AS. Printed by Ian Allan Printing Ltd, Riverdene Business Park, Hersham, Surrey KT12 4RG.

Code: 9905/E2

Front cover, inserts, top to bottom:
Controllers at work. *CAA*
Part of the UK low level chart of the Royal Air Force. *RAF*
AR3000 receiver. *AOR*

Front cover, lower:
Airbus A.310-304 of Air Portugal. *Author*

Back cover, top:
London, Heathrow Tower. *Author*

Back cover, bottom:
AR8200 Scanner. *AOR*

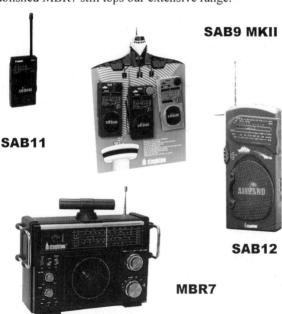

Introduction

Anyone considering the purchase of a receiver suitable for listening to messages between pilots and air traffic controllers will be faced with a bewildering array of high-tech equipment which has been made possible in recent years by advances in circuitry design and improvements in electronics. Some sets are quite expensive and many customers will be hesitant before parting with their money. Unfortunately, it is often difficult for the newcomer to arrive at a sensible decision, especially where the main area of interest is for aeronautical use. Often the sophisticated and comprehensive receiver which is commonplace today may well prove to be over specified, complicated to use and expensive.

This guide is for those readers who simply wish to have some impartial advice on what air traffic control transmissions are all about, and how to go about choosing a suitable receiver. Then, having decided upon the most appropriate piece of equipment, the book deals with the next question raised by most readers — how can we improve the reception of the messages by the use of external antennas, amplifiers and tuners?

Many aviation enthusiasts have no interest in radio as a subject — the ability to receive commands and responses between ground-based controllers and aircrew is desirable in order to understand and develop the hobby of aviation and airband listening. How this is achieved is of secondary importance, in the same way that someone choosing a television set needs no technical expertise on the theory of the subject.

Experience over many years of airband listening and numerous receivers has provided a wealth of practical knowledge which is passed on through this handbook. As with the first edition, I have been able to draw on the experiences of a great many people who regularly listen to aeronautical radio. Some of them are expert in the technology surrounding radio and associated subjects, but just as many are simply interested in the hobby of airband listening without having any particular knowledge of the technical side. In every case their comments and opinions have been greatly valued and hopefully this book will reflect this.

The manuscript for this book will have been completed many months prior to publication; much of the detail will, of course, be earlier than that. It is therefore inevitable that information on particular pieces of equipment may well be out of date by the time you come to read the book and it is essential, for this reason alone, that you check with your supplier before deciding on a purchase.

The variety of available airband scanners is changing so quickly that it is almost impossible to produce an up-to-date and meaningful guide covering individual models. Instead, the comments on receivers are of a general nature rather than being specific. The reception of ATC transmissions on VHF and UHF is determined by several factors: height above sea level; proximity of features which can restrict reception; type of antenna system employed; distance between the transmitter and the receiver; the sensitivity of the receiver; the strength of the signal and, last but not least, the weather.

In other words, the most expensive, sophisticated and sensitive receiver will produce very disappointing results if the location and the antenna system are inadequate. Conversely, a low cost general purpose set will give surprisingly good quality reception if it is located near to the transmitter — for example, when used at an airport or connected to a properly designed antenna system. On the other hand HF or Short Wave radio reception is not influenced to the same extent by these considerations. Long range reception can often be achieved with the simplest of antenna systems. Once a decision has been made the next question most people ask is about getting more from their receiver system and its associated components — the antenna, amplifiers and tuners. This will be covered as well later in the book.

In conclusion, this book is restricted to general advice on the principles of airband scanners, hopefully providing guidance and help on what to look for, in preference to actually comparing receiver A with receiver B. There are several other publications available which are eminently suitable reading for anyone who is interested in the technical aspects of radio.

Air Traffic Control in the UK

The United Kingdom and the Republic of Ireland are covered by regional Air Traffic Control centres which are entitled 'London', 'Scottish', 'Manchester' and 'Shannon'. These are located at West Drayton, a few miles north of Heathrow; at Prestwick in Ayrshire, Scotland; at Manchester International Airport; and at Shannon in Southern Ireland.

A significant area of northern England and the North Sea areas are covered by a special unit operating from Manchester Centre using the callsign 'Pennine Radar'.

The London and Scottish areas are known as Flight Information Regions (FIRs) and the Upper Airspace (above 24,500ft) as Upper Flight Information Regions (UIRs).

The London FIR extends across Wales and England to 55° North, approximately in line with Newcastle upon Tyne.

North of this line is the Scottish FIR which covers all of Scotland and Northern Ireland; both FIRs extend to the boundaries of the adjacent European FIRs to the south and east of the British Isles. The Scottish FIR covers a large area of the sea north of Scotland.

The Manchester centre covers a large area of central England up to FL195.

Except for Northern Ireland, Ireland's air traffic is handled by the Shannon FIR, with the control centre located at Shannon.

The Control System

Airspace in the United Kingdom is subdivided into several categories of service which vary in degree according to the kind of airspace in which the flight is operating. The levels of service range from the most basic to full mandatory control of air traffic where the controller is fully responsible for safe separation of aircraft.

Information Services

The simplest air traffic service is one in which pilots are given information concerning the local weather and details of other flights in the vicinity; the responsibility for remaining clear of other aircraft rests with the pilot. Any decisions to change level or heading will be at the discretion of the pilot, although the ATC unit will normally expect to be kept informed of any such manoeuvres. An Information Service will be non-radar, although sometimes it will be backed up by a radar unit, but as not all flights in the area may be seen on radar the service is often limited.

Information Services are provided for low-level general aviation flights routeing across the country, mostly in good visual conditions. Normally the service will be provided by local airfield controllers, either civil or military, complemented by a non-radar service given by the air traffic control centres in London and Scotland. These are known respectively as 'London Information' and 'Scottish Information'.

Advisory Services

An enhanced level of service is provided by a Radar Advisory Service, although the responsibility for remaining clear of other traffic still remains with the pilot.

The ATS unit will provide advice on other traffic to assist in avoiding other flights but the pilot does not have to accept that advice; therefore the decision as to what action to take is not that of the controller.

Radar Advisory Services are provided by a network of military and civilian airfields and also by the three centres to various flights operating outside controlled airspace.

Airways and Regulated Airspace

Regions of airspace in which the controller has responsibility for ensuring that air traffic is safely separated are referred to as Controlled Airspace. Pilots are only permitted to fly in such areas if they are qualified to fly on aircraft instruments, rather than visually. Pilots have to comply with instructions given by air traffic control regarding headings and changes of level.

Most controlled airspace in the UK is in the form of 'airways', usually 10-mile-wide corridors with a base level around 3,000ft and an upper limit of 24,500ft. The airway centre lines are based on straight lines between radio navigation beacons, and they link major airports and provide cross-country routes for intercontinental air traffic.

Upper Airspace

Above 24,500ft the whole of the airspace is subject to positive control, although the major routes still follow the same tracks set out by the airways in the lower airspace.

All airspace in the United Kingdom is categorised by a series of letters defined by the International Civil Aviation Organisation. The airspace which is subject to the highest degree of control is known as Class A airspace and this includes the system of airways which exist below FL245 (approximately 24,500ft).

All airspace above FL245 is Class B and aircraft are always subject to a control service.

At the moment there is no Class C airspace in the UK, but other classes (D, E, F and G) are in use and cover the entire country. The airspace with the least control is Class G which is also known as Free Airspace. However, none of these categories are referred to by pilots or air traffic controllers when talking to each other. The only phrases that are normally used are 'controlled' airspace or 'outside controlled' airspace.

Around airfields, aircraft at lower levels will be handled by controllers at the airfield itself, even though not all the flights will actually land at the airfield.

Oceanic Airspace

Over the North Atlantic an entirely different control system exists; this is because VHF radio waves are limited in range, and also because radar cover also depends on the line-of-sight principle.

Flights which are out of range of land — for example when crossing the North Atlantic — do not use VHF or UHF radio for communicating with the control centres. Instead, High Frequency (HF) radio is employed since this has an almost unlimited range, although it is less predictable in quality and reliability. However, the use of HF is gradually reducing as datalink via satellite becomes more widespread.

These systems allow the rapid and reliable transfer of information between aircraft and the ground and there is little doubt that HF radio will play only a small part in aviation in the future.

As the flights cannot be seen on radar, the control process is achieved by obtaining position reports from the aircrew on the position of the aircraft and comparing them with the flight plans to ensure that the required separation is maintained throughout the crossing.

The control centre for the eastern half of the North Atlantic region is located at Prestwick in Scotland but the actual messages from the aircraft are handled by a radio station at Ballygirreen, near Shannon in Ireland, from where they are sent by telex to Prestwick. Any replies from the control centre are transmitted to the aircraft by the Ballygirreen station.

Other areas of the North Atlantic are handled by separate centres based at Gander, Santa Maria, New York and Iceland.

Plans are already in hand for replacing the use of position reports and HF radio on busy oceanic routes with satellite-based air traffic control which will do away with the present system in many parts of the world, but probably not before 2010.

Trials with satellite communications have been continuing now for several years, but so far no firm implementation dates have been announced for the system to replace current arrangements.

Communications
The various levels and categories of the control process require the use of numerous radio frequencies and the new listener will probably have difficulty in following the variety of messages passing between pilots and controllers.

Radio messages from pilots can usually be heard reasonably well in most parts of the United Kingdom since aircraft at heights above 20,000ft will have a VHF radio range in excess of 150 miles. Unfortunately, however, since the radio waves depend on line-of-sight, communications from controllers may often be difficult to receive since the terrain can easily block transmissions from the various locations around the country where ATC aerials are located. A map showing the position of radio transmitters will give an indication of the likelihood of receiving messages satisfactorily. A good antenna system located as high as possible can often have a dramatic effect on the qualify of reception.

Further Reading
This brief introduction to the system of air traffic control in the United Kingdom has merely touched upon the outline of the very complex and ever-changing methods by which flights are handled by ground controllers.

If you would like to know more about the detail of the procedures and systems in use today you will probably find the companion publication *abc Air Traffic Control* useful.

Left:
Yupiteru VT 125 VHF receiver. *Waters & Stanton*

1 The Legal Position

Introduction

Generally, it is illegal to listen to transmissions on an airband receiver. However, this is an area of law which is often confusing for the public and it is common to hear incorrect statements and opinions.

Any apparatus designed for the receipt of aviation messages is considered to be an aeronautical station under the terms of the UK Air Navigation Order and as such requires the approval of the Civil Aviation Authority. The CAA, however, only recognises receiving stations that are required to provide an aeronautical service as being suitable for approval, therefore any other person or organisation will not be successful in applying for such authorisation.

A licence is not required for radio receiving apparatus (provided it is not capable of transmission) except that it is an offence to listen to so-called 'pirate' radio stations.

Anyone may legally own or sell a scanner but it may only be used for general reception, that is, public broadcasts such as Radio One, Radio Two, local radio stations, including the amateur band, Citizens Band Radio and marine weather and navigational information.

Listening to aeronautical transmissions is, therefore, an offence unless you have the authorisation from the Secretary of State.

The Law

The Air Navigation Order (ANO) and the Wireless Telegraphy Act 1949 both specifically prohibit the use of radio apparatus capable of receiving aeronautical messages — if you use, or intend to use, such equipment you can be prosecuted by the Civil Aviation Authority (through its agents) or the police under either or both sets of legislation. The police are becoming increasingly concerned about the number of scanners in use, particularly those which are used by criminals in order to monitor police frequencies and those which are used for the purpose of monitoring private telephone conversations. They have a certain degree of training in the use of scanners and are quite capable of examining a receiver to determine which frequencies are stored in the memories. If it is found that a particular frequency is stored in the memory the police may assume that the intention is to listen to that particular channel and could use this as evidence in a prosecution.

Two specific areas of law cover the position. The first, under Section 5(b) of the Wireless Telegraphy Act 1949, states that it is an offence if a person *'otherwise than under the authority of the Secretary of State or in his duty as a servant of the Crown, either (i) uses any wireless telegraphy apparatus with intent to obtain information as to the contents, sender or addressee of any message whether sent by means of wireless telegraphy or not, which neither the person using the apparatus nor any person on whose behalf he is acting is authorised by the Secretary of State to receive, or (ii) except in the course of any legal proceedings or for the purpose of any report thereof, discloses any information as to the contents, sender or addressee of any such message, being information which would not have come to his knowledge but for the use of wireless telegraphy apparatus by him or by another person.'*

In short, therefore, it is illegal to listen to anything other than general reception broadcasts, and it is also illegal to tell someone else what you have heard.

However, there is still some doubt concerning the attitude of the courts in reaching a decision in such cases. In the House of Lords on 4 June 1987 a case between *Rudd and The Secretary of State for Trade and Industry* resulted in a prosecution failing since the intent of the person involved was in doubt. Further cases as late as 1995 have followed the same principle.

Airband enthusiasts often ask if it is possible to obtain a licence for using a scanner. The answer is that licenses are not available other than for those persons acting at the request of the Secretary of State or on his behalf.

There is a common misunderstanding that it is acceptable to listen to non-broadcast messages provided the information is not passed on to anyone else. This is not correct. The offence is committed merely by listening in when not authorised to do so.

One of the latest and most sophisticated scanners which covers a very wide range of frequencies has a new feature, namely the inclusion of a bank of memories which require a password in order to gain access. Obviously this is intended for those frequencies which the listener wishes to remain confidential.

Going on Holiday?

Bear in mind that many foreign countries take a much more serious view of airband listening than Britain does, and even the sale of receivers capable of receiving air traffic control frequencies is prohibited.

Anyone considering taking a radio receiver abroad should be aware of the strictly applied regulations of some countries regarding unauthorised listening. At best, the authorities might confiscate the equipment. You might find yourself in serious trouble if you take your airband scanner to certain countries.

If any person chooses to disregard the law and listen to non-broadcast frequencies, then this must be at the risk of being found out and prosecuted.

Conclusion

At the present time, the authorities appear not to take very much interest in people who choose to listen to ATC frequencies, but there is a risk that a blatant disregard for the law may result in the position changing to the detriment of all those who pursue the hobby with no more than innocent interest.

Showing off your ability to receive the messages of controllers and pilots on your airband scanner could possibly result in everybody being penalised in the long run.

For more detailed information on the legal position, contact the Radio Communications Agency, New Kings Beam House, 22 Upper Ground, London SE1 9SA.

Right:
Steepletone SAB II air band receiver.
Waters & Stanton

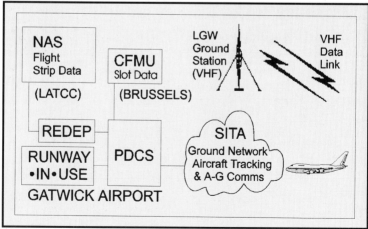

Above:
Some aircraft at Gatwick are given clearance by datalink instead of radio. In the diagram, NAS equals National Airspace System, CFMU equals Central Flow Management Unit, PDCS equals Pre-departure Clearance System and SITA equals Societé Internationale de Telecommunications Aéronautiques.
Civil Aviation Authority

2 What Can I Hear?

Aeronautical transmissions between controllers and aircrew can be received in most parts of the United Kingdom with one of the receivers listed later in the book. Some areas, however, will inevitably produce superior results for a variety of reasons. The main influence is the location of ATC transmitter sites which will have a significant effect on the quality of reception. Any transmissions from high flying aircraft will obviously be of much better quality since VHF radio operates on a line-of-sight principle.

The language used in ATC may at first be rather difficult to follow since the use of special words and phrases is commonplace, but with experience it will soon become easy to follow.

The countries of the world are generally covered by national aviation organisations, although oceanic areas are usually the responsibility of the countries at the perimeter. The national regions are known as Flight Information Regions.

Flight Information Regions

The United Kingdom and the Irish Republic form part of a European network of control areas with regions of control covering Scotland ('Scottish'), England and Wales ('London') and Ireland ('Shannon'). There is a separate centre based at Manchester Airport which covers a large area of central England up to Flight Level 195 (approximately 19,500ft). This centre uses the titles 'Manchester' and 'Pennine'.

England and Wales fall within a control area known as the London Flight Information Region, while Scotland is covered by another control area known as the Scottish Flight Information Region.

Within each Flight Information Region (FIR) the area is divided into several types of airspace — for example, airfields, airways, upper air routes, military training areas, danger areas and so on.

Air Traffic Services

Most, but not all, of the aircraft which fly in each of these separate kinds of airspace will be in radio contact with air traffic controllers whose function is to ensure maximum safety allied to the most expeditious flight profile. Certain kinds of airspace do not legally require radio communication between the aircraft and the ground.

Although they are usually referred to by the general term 'controllers', ATC personnel do not necessarily have direct control over the aircraft with which they are in contact.

According to the type of airspace in which the aircraft is flying the air traffic controller may be merely providing appropriate information or advice to the pilot, who must then decide on what action, if any, to take to remain safely clear of other nearby traffic. It is only in certain types of airspace that the controller becomes responsible for the proper separation of the flight — generally this is referred to as 'controlled' or regulated airspace. Flight crews must be suitably qualified and their aircraft must be technically equipped to certain prescribed standards before being allowed to operate in such areas.

Messages between controllers and flight crews vary in content according to the service being provided. Controllers messages are transmitted from numerous ground stations dotted all over the country. Most of these will be located at civil and military airfields, where the personnel will offer a service to flights using the airfield or passing through the area, whereas some are located at remote sites across the country, often operating from the same sites as radar transmitters.

As well as these 'local' operations, there will be numerous long-distance, high-flying aircraft criss-crossing the region en route to distant destinations. Many of these will be overflying the London or Scottish FIRs between the American continent and Europe.

ATC Centres

All high level flights and any other flights in one of the airways, are controlled from one of three Air Traffic Control centres. The centre for the London FIR is located at West Drayton (near Heathrow Airport), while the centre for the Scottish FIR is at Prestwick in Scotland. A separate centre operates from Manchester Airport for flights up to FL195.

The West Drayton Centre is due to be replaced by a new centre at Swanwick near Fareham in the next few years. A new Scottish centre is also planned.

Frequency Planning

Because VHF and UHF radio signals operate on a line-of-sight principle, it would not be practical to locate the transmitters for the whole of the UK at West Drayton or Prestwick — the effectiveness of the signals would be so poor that flights at the perimeter of the regions would be unable to receive the transmissions.

Due to the distances involved and the nature of VHF transmissions, it is necessary to locate the transmitters at strategic points throughout the country where they are able to provide the most effective radio cover to aircraft within their jurisdiction.

To avoid any possible interference and confusion between controllers and flight crews, the system is designed with separate radio frequencies for the different functions across the control areas, and the country is also divided into sectors of airspace both on plan and horizontally, with a separate group of controllers responsible for each sector.

The allocation of frequencies must be planned so that the same frequency is never used where it might be overheard by a controller or pilot for whom it is not intended. As it is possible to receive VHF or UHF signals at distances of up to 150 miles it requires careful planning across a region, and even between adjacent countries, to ensure that interference is minimised, if not eliminated.

There are hundreds of frequencies available for aeronautical use. In spite of this the organisers of European airspace are finding it increasingly difficult to plan the distribution of frequencies effectively.

Plans are well advanced for creating more capacity for VHF frequencies by further sub-division which will potentially treble the number of available channels. The busiest areas are sub-divided into smaller sectors, and therefore have more frequencies, and generally reception will be adequate in the south and southeast of England.

Furthermore, the relatively flat countryside means that the messages are uninterrupted by high ground as in other parts of the country.

Listeners who live in the more remote and rugged areas, such as North Wales and the Lake District, will undoubtedly suffer the problems of difficult and limited reception caused by high ground which blocks the line-of-sight. Also, there are fewer transmitters in these areas.

Controllers at airfields deal with low level flights close to the field — at most 50 miles away — therefore the transmitters they use are not required to be very high powered. It follows that an airband receiver which is beyond this distance will be unlikely to receive ground transmissions from airfields, although it is possible to improve reception greatly by the use of suitable aerials.

En-route high level flights are handled by civilian and military controllers at one of the centres mentioned earlier; each team of controllers has responsibility for a separate area (or sector) of airspace, with dedicated frequencies allocated to each of the sectors.

Radio transmitters for each centre are located on suitable sites remote from the centre, where they are able to provide the most efficient service to the flights in the area. Whereas the low powered equipment at airfields has to be effective only as far as local traffic is concerned, the en-route transmitters are more powerful with a greater range because all the flights dealt with are at relatively high level.

There are a limited number of en-route transmitters in the UK; listening to high level traffic on an airband receiver often results in messages from the aircraft being heard without difficulty, whereas the ATC responses are unlikely to be heard unless the receiver is somewhere in the vicinity of one of the transmitters.

Radio Frequencies

The frequency of a radio signal is measured in cycles per second; one cycle per second is known as a HERTZ; one thousand cycles per second is referred to as one KILO-hertz, and one million cycles per second is known as one MEGA-hertz. Thus, one thousand kilohertz (kHz) is the same as one megahertz (MHz). For example, one popular frequency used by flights crossing the North Atlantic is '5649'. This is either 5649kHz or (more properly) 5.649MHz or in other words 5MHz and 649kHz.

All the frequencies used between air traffic controllers and aircrew are in megahertz, grouped into three blocks. The lowest frequency is 2MHz, the highest 400MHz. More details on this are given later.

The way in which frequencies are quoted can sometimes be confusing. Shortwave frequencies used by flights over the North Atlantic for example are given in kilohertz (kHz) which means they consist of four or five figures (eg 8864 or 10069). However, receiver specifications normally state the range of frequencies in megahertz (MHz) — in these cases the range falls between 8 and 11MHz.

For example, a receiver which is advertised as having a range between 150kHz and 60MHz is the same as saying that the receiver covers 0.15MHz to 60MHz or, alternatively, 150kHz to 60,000kHz.

Aeronautical Frequency Bands

The frequencies used for aviation messages are grouped as follows:

High Frequency (Shortwave)

This is used where it is necessary to pass messages over long distances. The range is between 2MHz and 23MHz, although not every frequency is allocated for aeronautical purposes. Groups of frequencies within the range are designated to other uses. This group is sometimes called 'Short Wave' but the modern term is High Frequency, abbreviated to 'HF' by controllers and pilots alike. The use of HF for aeronautical purposes is declining with the advent of datalink and satellites providing ATC with much more accurate and reliable communications with aircraft.

Very High Frequency

Civil flights and certain military flights transmitting across short distances — perhaps

100 miles or so — will use frequencies between 118MHz and 136.975MHz. This group is referred to as Very High Frequency or VHF. Some pilots, especially those on military flights, describe the VHF range as 'Victor' frequencies.

Ultra High Frequency
Military flights transmitting over distances of around 100 miles or so (the same distances as for VHF) are allocated frequencies in a range between 225MHz and 400MHz. This group is known as Ultra High Frequency or UHF, often known as 'Uniform' frequencies to pilots.

Navigation Frequencies
There are certain other frequencies outside these ranges which are used for other specialist purposes, mainly navigation beacons, instrument landing systems and so on. These are between 108MHz and 117.950MHz in 50kHz spacings.

Repeater Frequencies
Another group of frequencies (455.475-455.975MHz Narrow Band FM) are used as repeater stations at airfields for use by ground operational staff who are able to listen to ATC instructions at the same time as communicating with each other. These frequencies are not normally available on a dedicated airband scanner.

Choosing a Receiver
There is a trend towards wide band scanners in preference to dedicated sets which in some ways has an effect on the quality of reception for each particular range of frequencies. Often the listener will not be too interested in the huge spectrum of frequencies available on a wide band receiver and it has to be asked whether the airband listener really benefits from the purchase of one of these modern pieces of equipment. Generally speaking the best results will be obtained from a receiver which is designed for a specific range of frequencies (airband for example) rather than from a wide band model.

Most newcomers to the hobby of airband listening buy a receiver suitable for the second group of frequencies, which is the one used by all civilian aircraft. They are likely to be the least expensive, readily available (particularly on the secondhand market), give good results and (important for beginners) the number of messages on individual frequencies is far greater than with any other aeronautical band.

Although the density of traffic varies considerably in different parts of the country, listening to transmissions on VHF can often result in an almost continuous stream of messages during the day.

Some VHF receivers are also capable of receiving transmissions on the third group of frequencies (the Ultra High Frequency or UHF range) in addition to VHF. Receivers for UHF exclusively are not normally available — but check with your supplier first.

The extent of military transmissions on the UHF band is far less than is usually experienced with civilian air traffic on VHF. This is partly because there are a very much larger number of available frequencies (if every frequency between 225MHz and 400MHz were in use at 25kHz spacings there would be 7,000 channels!) and partly because military aviation transmissions are allocated frequencies not only related to the location of the flight but also the function of the flight. In other words, the kind of

Below:
AOR AR5000 air band receiver. *AOR*

11

task the aircraft is performing often determines the frequency to be used irrespective of the area in which it is working.

Military flights tend to operate mostly during weekday periods; the number of flights taking place during the night and at weekends is very much reduced.

High Frequency (Short Wave)
The transmissions on the first group of frequencies (High Frequency) can only be received on a certain type of receiver, and because the principles involved are quite different from those used for VHF and UHF the subject is dealt with separately in Chapter 6.

There are now several hand held receivers on the market which cover all three aeronautical ranges.

Finding the Information
All the frequencies in use for air traffic control purposes in the UK are readily available to the public by a variety of means. Apart from those official publications which are produced for the aviation world, there are also several manuals specifically intended to give ATC enthusiasts the detail they require in an easy to understand style.

Two kinds of official publication cover aviation and aeronautical radio. First there are charts used for air navigation purposes, covering individual airfields, airways, high level air routes, oceanic areas and terminal control areas; some have the principal radio communication frequencies printed on the sheet. Of course, the frequencies on the individual sheets are limited to those which relate directly to the area covered by the chart, so to obtain full coverage of all frequencies necessitates the purchase of a great number of charts, obviously an expensive exercise.

The second official group of publications from which frequencies can be obtained are known as the *Communications Supplements*, published by the Royal Air Force or by Aerad. Each organisation produces its own version, both being very similar in content. They cover a great amount of detail about aviation procedures, as well as frequencies, but they are a little on the expensive side for the amateur. However, out of date issues can often be purchased for much less.

There are numerous books produced specifically for this purpose. Several publications specialise in providing very detailed listings of VHF and UHF aeronautical radio frequencies, usually classified into airfields, airways and other useful categories such as 'company' frequencies. None of the official publications provide the same level of detail as these specialist books, so they are probably a 'best buy' as far as total coverage is concerned.

Most of the frequencies in use in UK airspace are listed at the end of this book, although it is inevitable that some of these will have been superseded by the time of publication, especially in view of the changes involving the reduction in channel spacing.

Of course, some pilots have difficulty in being aware of the new frequencies. There is no problem with this, because every change of frequency is notified to the pilot by the controller, who will be fully conversant with any changes. The airband listener can adopt the same approach, listening out for new frequencies given out by the air traffic controllers over the radio. Experienced airband enthusiasts will quickly spot any new frequencies as soon as they arise; their need for official publications on frequency changes is therefore very limited.

What Can I Hear?
First time listeners to an airband receiver are likely to be bewildered by the various transmissions they hear; some of the messages will not be concerned with Air Traffic Control. Many of the 760 channels on VHF and the 7,000 on UHF are allocated to several categories of service provided by ATC in terms of positive control, advice or simply information, depending on the circumstances.

Obviously the primary allocations are for transmissions between flights and controllers, perhaps locally where airfield conditions prevail, or 'en-route' for high level traffic under the control of a major control centre.

The transmissions will be in one of the following categories:

Radio Navigation Beacons
These are Very High Frequency Omni-Directional Radio (VOR) or Doppler Very High Frequency Omni-Directional Radio (DVOR). These are the main navigation facilities located at important points on airways. The identity of the beacon is transmitted in morse code, continuously throughout the day and night, on the frequency indicated on radio navigation charts. The name of each of the beacons is known as its 'designator' — for example, Clacton VOR in Essex is designated Charlie Lima November (CLN) and transmits on frequency 114.55MHz.

All VHF beacons operate on frequencies between 108MHz and 117.950MHz. They are listed in the appendices.

'Volmet' Broadcasts
There are four VHF frequencies which continuously broadcast current details for UK airfields, each of which gives a variety of information about airfield conditions.

The information provided in this way is known as 'VOLMET', and the broadcasts cover the following locations:

■ London Volmet Main — Frequency 135.375 — Amsterdam, Brussels, Dublin, Glasgow, London Gatwick, London Heathrow, London Stansted, Manchester, Paris Charles De Gaulle.

■ London Volmet South — Frequency 128.6 — Birmingham, Bournemouth, Bristol, Cardiff, Jersey, Luton, Norwich, Southampton, Southend.

■ London Volmet North — Frequency 126.6 — Blackpool, East Midlands, Isle of Man, Leeds/Bradford, Liverpool, London Gatwick, Manchester, Newcastle, Teesside.

■ Scottish Volmet — Frequency 125.725 — Aberdeen, Belfast/Aldergrove, Edinburgh, Glasgow, Inverness, London Heathrow, Prestwick, Stornoway, Sumburgh.

■ Shannon Volmet — European airports are covered by a similar service, on high frequency radio, known as Shannon Volmet. Details are given in the chapter covering HF radio.

■ Royal Air Force Volmet — This service provides details for all European military airfields which are used by the RAF. This is broadcast on HF radio and details are given in the HF chapter.

The broadcasts are compiled from pre-recorded voice segments which cover all possible combinations of weather conditions. These are automatically linked together by computer to give a very realistic continuous message for each airport covered. The broadcasts are continuous throughout the day and night, with automatic updating as new details of conditions are received.

Automatic Terminal Information Services (ATIS)
Many of the larger airfields in the UK broadcast details of local weather conditions on a continuous basis on specific frequencies; these are published in various documents relating to airfield facilities, details of which are covered in the appendices.

The popular airfields with continuously broadcast information are listed, but by the time this book is published some of the frequencies may have been changed and other locations will probably have been added. Small airports will not be provided with a dedicated airport information frequency; instead the weather and other relevant details will be passed, on request, by ATC personnel to individual flights.

As airfields become increasingly busy the 'air time' taken by controllers in reading out weather details reaches a level whereby an alternative method becomes essential. The solution is to provide a separate frequency used purely for the continuous broadcast of local conditions. (It should be noted that 'continuous' may not mean that the full 24hr will be covered. In some cases, the transmission times may only be, for example, between 09.00 and 21.00 UTC.)

Airfield information transmissions are known as 'ATIS' (Automatic Terminal Information Services). The message is preceded by a letter (for example 'Hotel'). The broadcast will continue on a repetitive basis until one of the aspects included in the message is changed. The revised information will then be broadcast in an updated format prefixed with the next letter of the alphabet — in this case 'India'.

When pilots first contact the airfield they are able to identify the information they have obtained on their second radio by reference to the particular letter — for example, *'Information India received'*.

Company Frequencies
It is essential that aircraft crews are able to make contact with their operating bases on dedicated radio frequencies rather than pass messages through the channels used for ATC purposes. In fact, controllers will usually refuse to handle non-ATC messages (except, of course, in an emergency) but will instead request the caller to select one of the frequencies notified for such use.

The major airlines will have at least one frequency in the UK for company use. Virtually all company frequencies are in a range between 129MHz and 132MHz, although by no means every channel will be used for this purpose. A small number of company frequencies are contained within the band between 136MHz and 136.975MHz.

Programming a scanner to search between 129.00 and 132.00 will usually provide several company channels which may not be listed in frequency publications.

Smaller airlines, which are not based in the UK or which choose not to establish their own base station, may use the company facilities of one of the larger airlines or a specialist handling company such as Servisair.

Company transmissions generally concern flight departure times, arrival times, passenger numbers, requests for wheelchairs, medical assistance, technical advice and so forth.

Some of the frequently used company channels are listed in the appendices.

Gliders, Microlights, Hang-gliders, Balloons and Parachutists

Each of these categories of flight has been allocated VHF radio frequencies so that pilots may communicate with each other and with their bases. These are as follows:

- Gliders   129.90
- Hang-gliders   129.90
- Balloons   129.90
- Parachutists   130.30

En-route Traffic

The United Kingdom is the main gateway to the North Atlantic for European air traffic, with a significant proportion of traffic overflying the region at high levels. These flights are controlled from West Drayton or Prestwick on VHF or UHF frequencies reserved for the major air routes. The same frequencies are used for internal UK flights using the airways system or the upper air routes. As flights cross the country they pass from one sector to the next and each time this occurs there will be a frequency change given by the controller.

The current published frequencies are listed in the appendices.

Most of the frequencies within this category will be transmitted on the 'offset' principle, which is described in Chapter 7.

Shanwick Oceanic Clearances

Before a flight is permitted to enter the airspace of the North Atlantic it is a requirement that ATC clearance is obtained. Pilots can be heard on one of three VHF frequencies requesting Oceanic Clearance from the Oceanic Control Centre at Prestwick. (The particular frequency used by the flight is related to its country of origin.)

The frequencies currently in use are 123.95MHz, 127.65MHz and 135.52MHz.

The ATC responses are transmitted from Dundonald Hill (Scotland) and Davidstow Moor (Cornwall). Therefore, unless the receiver is located in a position within reasonable distance of one of these transmitters the controller will not normally be heard on an airband receiver.

North Atlantic Tracks

The tracks themselves vary on a daily basis. They are identified by a letter with westbound tracks commencing with Track Alpha as the most northerly, and eastbound tracks using Track Zulu as the most southerly. Track information for westbound tracks is given an identification number representing the day of the year, starting with 001 on 1 January. Details of track allocations are sent to airlines by a system of teleprinter networks.

Information and Advisory Services

Flights outside controlled or regulated airspace may request an information service on one of several frequencies for London or Scottish airspace as detailed in the appendices.

These services are 'procedural', ie not assisted by radar, so the degree of service is limited. Also, due to staffing difficulties, the availability of controllers providing the service from the Scottish or London ATC centres is restricted.

Other services include radar information and radar advice under the LARS system (Lower Airspace Radar Service). A series of airfields both military and civilian provide a network of cover over most, but not all, of the United Kingdom.

Local Airfields

Most airfields in the UK are allocated two or more radio frequencies for dealing with air traffic arriving at or departing the airfield, or for those flights overflying the airfield within the jurisdiction of the local ATC unit.

The control of traffic landing or taking off is handled by controllers in the Visual Control Room on the 'Tower' frequency. Flights away from the airfield itself will be dealt with by the 'Approach' Controller, usually assisted by radar. The Approach Controller will usually handle outbound traffic as well as inbound flights.

Busier airfields may be provided with separate 'Ground' and 'Clearance Delivery' frequencies, dealing with the movement of all traffic on the runways and taxiways, and also flight plan clearances.

At military airfields there are even more sub-divisions, each related to the type of service being provided. Often different military frequencies are referred to as 'studs', a term used to indicate pre-set frequencies which can be chosen instantly by the pilot by selecting the appropriate button or 'stud' on the radio.

Most military airfields also have a range of VHF frequencies for those flights which are not provided with UHF radio.

Large and complicated airports such as Heathrow have several other frequencies, each allocated to specific tasks within the airport structure, enabling the airfield to operate smoothly and safely. Complex airports simply could not function with only two or three frequencies in use.

Fire Service Vehicles
Virtually all airport fire service vehicles operate on frequency 121.6MHz (VHF) when within the airfield boundary.

Distress and Diversion
Aircraft which are in trouble of any kind — for example, lost with engine trouble or any other emergency situation — can contact the Distress and Diversion unit at the control centres of West Drayton or Prestwick on the international emergency frequencies of 121.5MHz (VHF) or 243MHz (UHF).

In fact, flights which are already under the control of an air traffic control unit will report their problem to the controller on the frequency which they are currently using; the distress frequencies are normally used by aircraft outside regulated airspace.

Above:
One of the sector suites at the London at West Drayton. *Civil Aviation Authority*

The popular name given to the Distress and Diversion call (D and D) is *'Mayday'*. There are in fact two levels of emergency — *'Mayday'* is for flights in real distress, whereas the lower level of distress, known as *'Pan'* is for flights which need assistance or guidance without the urgency of a full-scale emergency situation.

Pilots can often be heard on the distress frequency simulating emergencies with the radio call *'Practise Pan'* — *'Practise Pan — Practise Pan'*. This gives pilots and controllers an opportunity to practise real life situations without the urgency of real time situations. Obviously if a genuine emergency arises during the practice, that will immediately take precedence.

For pilots wishing to confirm their position, a separate 'fixer' service is available through the distress and diversion cell, using the same frequencies.

A pilot in distress will use the callsign 'Mayday', spoken three times, or alternatively the callsign 'Pan Pan', also spoken three times.

The possibility of hearing a distress message is, in fact, quite rare. The receiver can be tuned to the emergency frequency for hours at a time without a single transmission being heard. The most likely way to detect such messages is by the use of a voice-activated tape recorder — details of such systems are covered in Chapter 7.

On average there will be one or two emergency situations every day in the United Kingdom.

3 Features For VHF/UHF Receivers

This chapter briefly covers the various facilities provided on many of the radio receivers available today. More detailed information is given in Chapter 4.

Scanners

This is a general term used to describe a receiver which is either capable of automatically switching from one specific memorised channel to another, often at high speed, in order to detect any transmissions which may be taking place on any of the memorised frequencies, or which can search across all the available frequencies regardless of the memorised channels. If a transmission is detected the scanning/searching stops. When the transmission is over, the scan continues, although the receivers can be set to remain indefinitely on the frequency on which the initial transmission was received.

Scanning usually refers to the receiver systematically stepping through the memorised frequencies programmed into the receiver by the user. Only those frequencies stored in the memory are checked during the scanning operation.

Searching

This term describes the ability of the receiver to step rapidly through all the frequencies, either on VHF or UHF, stopping when a transmission (or any other source of sound) is heard. Usually the search commences at the lowest frequency and proceeds through the entire range to the highest frequency, after which the process is repeated. Many scanners also have a facility of searching between any two specified frequencies chosen by the listener. The ability to search has obvious advantages, allowing the listener to find and record unknown and little used frequencies. It is particularly helpful when locating 'company' frequencies, which are almost all confined to 80 channels on the VHF band between 130.00kHz and 132.00kHz. By programming the scanner to search between these two limits any company transmissions will be detected. As many of the frequencies are used only occasionally this can be an efficient and rewarding way of finding the transmissions.

Pass (or Lockout)

Often, during a scanning or searching operation, the receiver will lock onto a frequency which is giving a continuous unwanted transmission. The receiver will therefore stop at the particular frequency and will remain there until the instruction is given to continue the search/scan.

Where unwanted signals are being received, a pass facility will enable any specific frequency to be eliminated from the process of scan or search.

Any frequency locked out can be reinstated just as easily at the press of the appropriate key.

Hand-helds

A modern self-explanatory expression, describing receivers which are completely portable. They will be battery powered, of small dimensions, with a simple antenna supplied with the receiver.

Modern technology ensures a sophisticated and comprehensive range of facilities, even in the smallest sets.

Some receivers can be plugged into the electrical circuit of a car, via the cigarette lighter socket, as an alternative to using batteries, or from the mains via a transformer. Another option is to use rechargeable batteries which can be recharged from mains power, sometimes without the need to remove the batteries from the set.

'Hand-helds' are mainly VHF or VHF/UHF, making them particularly suitable for use at airfields or at airshows, but there are also a number of hand-held receivers capable of receiving all three aeronautical frequency ranges — VHF, UHF and HF.

Base Stations

These receivers are normally kept at a permanent location, invariably mains operated, and with an antenna system far superior to the portable type used with 'hand-helds'. Usually the receiver is of a 'table-top' design with a large keypad for frequency entries and a large clear display for the actual frequencies.

A modern trend is to combine the functions of 'hand-helds' and base stations into one versatile receiver which can meet the requirements of both types. Many receivers can be operated from any type of power source with any type of antenna connected to it. Specially designed stands incorporating a recharging unit are available to support the hand-held set when used as a base station, helping to overcome the problem of small lightweight sets remaining upright and at the same time easy to operate.

Squelch Control

Virtually all good quality VHF or UHF receivers are provided with a 'squelch' control, a device which is adjusted to eliminate the continuous background noise which can be heard between messages. When a transmission takes place the squelch is automatically opened.

Frequency Steps

Until several years ago the separation between frequencies on both VHF and UHF airbands was 50kHz — for example, 127.000MHz, 127.050, 127.100, 127.150, etc.

Because of the need to increase the number of available channels on VHF it was then decided (in 1976) to double the number of frequencies by reducing the separation to 25kHz, thereby giving twice the range for VHF operations. The examples quoted earlier therefore became 127.000MHz, 127.025, 127.050, 127.075 and so on. In 1992 the separation between UHF frequencies was also reduced from 50kHz to 25kHz.

8.33kHz Channel Spacings

The current congestion within the VHF range of frequencies for civil aeronautical radio in Europe has resulted in proposals to sub-divide the channel spacing between different frequencies from the present 25kHz down to spacings of 8.33kHz thereby trebling the number of available channels. The new arrangement will initially only affect the southeast of the United Kingdom, probably only the London Upper Sector which deals with high level over-flights.

Since October 1998 it has been mandatory for flight plans to include details of radio equipment carried on-board the aircraft in order to assess the rate at which airline operators are installing the new receiving equipment.

On 7 October, 1999, the carriage of 8.33kHz radio sets will become mandatory in European airspace for all flights operating above FL245 (or FL195 over France).

It is currently planned to introduce the new spacings in UK airspace in June 2000, but this is yet to be confirmed.

After October 1999 only aircraft fitted with two operational receivers capable of handling the new 8.33 spacings will be permitted to fly in upper airspace over Europe. Also, where an 8.33 channel is allocated in a particular sector of airspace, no alternative 25kHz frequency will be available.

The 8.33 spacings will initially be implemented for operational use in the upper airspace of Austria, Belgium, France, Germany, Luxembourg, the Netherlands and Switzerland. However, the carriage of the equipment will apply to all European states.

Traffic which is flight-planned to operate in the upper airspace will not be permitted to descend below FL245 (FL195 over France) in order to avoid a sector using the new channel spacings.

There will be a few exceptions to the requirements, mainly covering state aircraft, medical flights and Search and Rescue traffic.

It will not be possible to operate the two systems in the same area because of the risk of interference which could prevent messages being received by ATC or by pilots.

Below:
The high-level sector of airspace over London and southeast England will be the first to switch to the new 8.33 channel spacing. *Civil Aviation Authority*

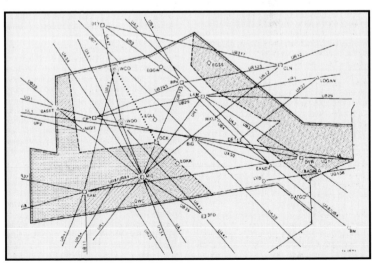

It will, therefore, be necessary to reallocate a number of frequencies in the southeast of England where the system will initially be implemented in order to avoid overlaps.

The new range of frequencies (which will be known by a new term 'Channels') will be separated by 8.33kHz. However, in order to simplify radio telephony procedures they will be given 5kHz descriptions as shown in the table.

A special Frequency Management Plan has been devised by the Eurocontrol drafting group responsible for planning the changes. The plan is necessary to ensure that no interference problems will be encountered. The transition to 8.33kHz channel spacing, will depend on a number of the current 25kHz frequencies being moved out of the bands which are intended to accommodate the new spacings. Most of the new frequencies within the 8.33kHz spacings will be accommodated in the band between 132.00 and 134.80, therefore existing frequencies in the 25kHz spacings will need to be reallocated. It is anticipated that at least 70 frequencies will have to be changed by the year 2000. As the range of VHF transmissions is in the order of 200 miles, this will be a major undertaking for the authorities.

A few scanners are now available which are specifically designed to cope with the new spacings and these will enable the user to search through the airband in increments of 8.33kHz. However, the receiver has to be designed so that the actual tuning arrangement provides steps of 8.33, 16.66 and 00.00. Some receivers may not be able to accept these steps, therefore searching may not be successful as the receiver will go out of tune.

This does not mean that in order to listen to the new channels it will be essential to have a receiver with these specific steps. If you are aware of the actual frequency being used (they will be available in many of the publications available through the Royal Air Force, Aerad, etc.) it will be possible to tune the receiver to the actual frequency provided the receiver is fitted with steps of 1kHz or below. The frequency can then be stored in the scanner's memory for future use. It is only in the search mode that 8.33kHz spacings become essential.

Most transmissions operate at around 5kHz above or below the published frequency and these can be received quite adequately on most of the modern scanners. So, for example, tuning to a frequency of 132.083 by entering 132.08 or 132.09 should produce satisfactory results.

In the section covering scanners the ability to tune a particular set to the new range of channels is indicated in the description. Essentially only those scanners which do not have steps of less than 5kHz will present a problem.

Radio Telephony Procedures

There are internationally agreed procedures for describing VHF or UHF aeronautical radio frequencies.

Where the frequency consists of six characters, the last digit is never spoken. Also if the fifth digit happens to be zero, it is not spoken. The following examples should clarify the correct phraseology:

■ 127.100 is spoken as 'one two seven decimal one'
■ 135.375 is spoken as 'one three five decimal three seven'
■ 118.050 is spoken as 'one one eight decimal zero five'

Throughout this book frequencies may be given as five or six digit numbers but the above rules will always apply.

Frequency Range

Every receiver will have a range of frequencies specified by the manufacturer. Unless otherwise stated, it may be assumed that the range between the lowest and highest frequency will be 'continuous' — that is to say there will be no gaps. If there are any gaps, then this must be stated by the manufacturer.

Unfortunately, some airband receivers are still advertised as (for example) being suitable for UHF/VHF, whereas in fact the complete range of frequencies is not covered.

Another point to bear in mind is the incorrect frequency range often published for a particular receiver, sometimes to the disadvantage of the manufacturer! It is not uncommon to see a published top frequency of 136.00MHz for a VHF receiver whereas in fact the range extends beyond 137.00MHz.

One further area of interest for the airband listener is the repeater frequencies used at airports. These are Personal Mobile Radio channels in the Narrow FM range which enable airport staff (ground engineers, fire crews, vehicle drivers, police, etc) to listen to messages from Air Traffic Control and aircraft.

They operate on the duplex system; that is, the base station and the mobile transceiver send and receive messages on different frequencies.

Many airband scanners are not provided with NFM mode, therefore tuning in to these channels will not be possible, but this should not deter one from purchasing a particular receiver since the additional interest is very limited.

Frequencies are usually in the 453.0000 to 456.0000MHz range. Details for individual airports are given in specialist scanning handbooks.

Below:
When the new 8.33kHz spacing is introduced, a new term ('channel') will be used in radiotelephony messages. This is an example of some of the new frequencies. *Eurocontrol*

Spacing (kHz)	Frequencies (MHz)	25 kHz mode "frequency"	8.33 kHz mode "channel"
25	132,0000	132,00	
8.33	132,0000		132,005
8.33	132,0083		132,010
8.33	132,0166		132,015
25	132,0250	132,02	
8.33	132,0250		132,030
8.33	132,0333		132,035
8.33	132,0416		132,040
25	132,0500	132,05	

Below:
Diagram indicating the terms used at airfields.
Author

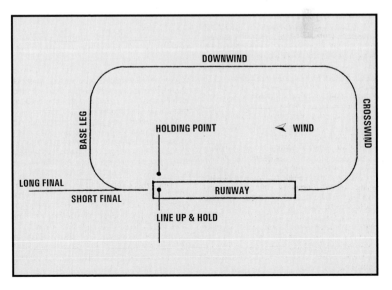

4 What to Look For in a VHF/UHF Receiver

Prospective purchasers may find it useful to have a basic understanding of the terms used by the manufacturers and suppliers of radio receivers suitable for airband use.

Advertisements are often a maze of very descriptive phrases which, at first glance, give the impression that one particular model must surely be the best value and the most comprehensive. Sometimes, in fact, the essential detail for the airband listener may be difficult to determine, so before rushing to the telephone to place your order consider carefully what it is you actually want and then check by asking specific questions about the performance of the particular model. This is especially important if your interest is confined to the aeronautical radio frequencies used by civilian and military flights which only use VHF and UHF.

There are many excellent sets available on the secondhand market, and purchases made this way are likely to give outstanding value for money. The only drawback is that you will not usually be able to return the set if it turns out to be unsuitable for your purpose. On the other hand you are likely to get some specific comments on the performance of the set from the seller. Many of the receivers described in the appendicies are available only on the secondhand market.

A few retail outlets do agree to give a full refund if the receiver turns out to be inadequate, for whatever reason, provided, of course, it is returned in perfect condition within a specified time. Some shops have a sample set which can be loaned to prospective purchasers on a trial basis.

One well-known high street store has a policy of accepting returns without question. In effect this means having a scanner on a trial basis before deciding whether to keep that particular model.

It is very easy to assume from technical specifications, full of detailed statistics, that the scanner is capable of receiving virtually all that the airband enthusiast can ever require. Careful examination might reveal, however, that although the characteristics of the particular receiver might well be superb, it does not necessarily mean that the frequencies cover the entire airband range, or that performance in the airband channels give the best results.

Some sets are said to cover 'VHF and UHF airbands' whereas in fact there can be gaps in the frequencies which can actually be received.

Sometimes the same model receiver produced by the same manufacturer at different times may have an updated range of frequencies on the later model. Also sets on sale abroad may not be equipped to the same standard as UK models since airband frequencies are illegal in many parts of the world, so beware of unbelievable special offers.

The advice, therefore, is to be quite specific in your questions as to what the new purchase will actually do — ask the seller to state categorically whether each of the requirements is provided.

Civilian VHF

The frequencies which are essential in the VHF voice range start at 108.000MHz at the lower end and 136.975MHz at the top end, in 'steps' of 25kHz — this means that individual frequencies are separated by 25kHz, the standard spacing between VHF frequencies used throughout the world for civilian air traffic control transmissions. For example, 134.450 is separated from adjacent frequencies by 25kHz, giving 134.475 and 134.425, the channels above and below 134.450. A separate range of frequencies between 108.000 and 117.975MHz cover radio navigation beacons.

25kHz is the international separation between VHF frequencies fitted to aeronautical radio receivers in civil aircraft, and virtually all modern scanners are capable of selecting the separate channels. Dedicated VHF airband receivers generally give very good results, usually superior to wide-band scanners.

June 2000 is the proposed date for the introduction of new VHF channels in the United Kingdom. These will be separated by 8.33kHz instead of the present 25kHz, thus increasing threefold the number of available frequencies.

For example, instead of stepping from 132.00 to 132.025, the new steps will be 132.00, 132.0083, 132.0166 and then 132.025.

Some scanners on the market in 1999 already provide the 8.33 facility. However, it is not necessary to own one of these in order to receive the new channels.

Most modern sets can be programmed with steps as low as 1kHz. Some have even smaller steps. These scanners can have the new range of frequencies entered and memorised closely enough for perfectly adequate reception.

It is also important to remember that the introduction of new channels will be limited. Firstly, they will only apply to upper airspace above FL245, and secondly, only the southeast of England will be affected. Chapter 3 describes the new system in more detail.

Summary: Frequencies must be between 118.000 and 136.975MHz. Steps are to be 25kHz as a minimum, but with steps of 1kHz to cope with the new 8.33 channel spacings.

Military UHF

If your interest is in the military side of aviation, you might wish to consider the purchase of a receiver which is specifically designed to receive aeronautical transmissions between 225MHz and 400MHz. There are a number of models on the market which are described as being suitable for military use, but a careful check is advised before a decision is made since not all receivers are capable of covering the complete military band. In fact, a few scanner advertisements which claim suitability for military use are actually misleading since only part of the range of frequencies is provided.

Take care to ensure that the set in question does have the full cover between 225 and 400MHz at 25kHz spacings.

Also, remember that military air traffic messages tend to be far fewer than those on the civil frequencies; at weekends, bank holidays and during the night the volume of military air traffic is considerably reduced, and there are likely to be long periods of silence between transmissions.

Military ATC does not operate in the same way as the civilian system, therefore listening to transmissions is far less predictable. Unless you are close to an active military airfield you may well be disappointed.

There are several military frequencies used for civil flights which take place, in fact, on VHF, being operated by London or Scottish Military Control. In addition, military flights which are using the normal airways system will do so under the control of the civil air traffic controllers on the normal VHF channels.

Variable Frequency Spacing

Most airband receivers are designed to operate at frequencies which are 'stepped' (ie separated) by 25kHz, the normal spacing used in aviation voice transmissions.

For technical reasons, ATC messages for high flying en-route civil or military traffic are often transmitted on channels which are slightly higher or lower than the published frequency. The actual transmission can be 2.5, 5.0 or 7.5kHz higher or lower than the promulgated frequency quoted in ATC documentation.

If your scanner is receiving signals from a transmitter operating on one of these frequencies it is possible that reception will be improved if the receiver can be tuned to a frequency slightly higher or slightly lower than the published one, so that it matches precisely the actual transmission.

If the signals are strong, the offset will not have any effect on reception, but if the signals are weak (due perhaps to the distance between the receiver and the transmitter) the slight difference can improve matters considerably.

It is a positive advantage to have a receiver provided with a facility for selecting a frequency higher or lower than the published one.

An alternative use for this feature is to 'tone down' a particularly strong and distorted signal from a transmitter located near to the receiver.

Some of the latest scanners can be programmed to step down as low as 1kHz or as high as 999kHz so that the user can select any frequency across the entire range with an accuracy of 1kHz.

For practical purposes, however, the ability to tune in 5kHz increments gives good results and is available on many modern receivers.

Summary: The facility to select 5kHz steps (or even lower) is a positive advantage, especially in those areas remote from the transmitter stations.

Memories

Most modern airband receivers are capable of storing a number of frequencies, ranging from 10 to 1,000. This feature simply ensures that those frequencies chosen by the listener can be stored in the receiver's memory, ready for selection whenever needed.

Naturally, the ability to store frequencies has no effect on the quality of reception of the individual receiver — it merely makes the selection of frequencies much more convenient and relieves the listener of the chore of entering separate channels each time they are needed.

For example, airband scanners provided with 100 memory channels usually have 10 'banks', or groups, each of 10 memories. These can conveniently be used for separate purposes, ie VHF en-route frequencies, UHF frequencies, 'company', local airfields, Heathrow, Gatwick and so on. As each bank can be monitored independently this facility has obvious advantages.

A receiver provided with a memory facility can also be used with another function, known as 'scanning' which is covered next.

Summary: All modern receivers have memories. choose a set with an adequate number of memory channels for your purpose.

Scanning

Any frequency stored in the memory of a receiver can be monitored to check whether any transmission is taking place. If a signal is detected, the receiver will remain on the individual frequency for as long as the signal is transmitted, after which the receiver continues to check all memorised frequencies in turn for the next transmission. The ability to carry out this process is referred to as 'scanning' or occasionally 'memory scanning'. Receivers with this facility are described as 'scanners'.

Most receivers that are able to scan are also

provided with a choice for the listener when using the scanning feature. It is possible to decide, when a signal is detected on a particular frequency, whether to remain on that frequency indefinitely even though the transmissions have ceased (known as 'Hold') or whether to continue the scan after a predetermined interval. It is also a common feature to be able to delay the period before scanning restarts. When the scan is set to 'Hold', the receiver will stop scanning once a signal is detected and will remain on that frequency indefinitely until the user decides to continue the scan. If the scan is set to 'Delay', the receiver will cease the scanning process once a signal is detected. It will then remain on that frequency until the transmission has ended, after which it will stay on the frequency for a few seconds, waiting for any further transmissions. If no such signal is detected the scan will be resumed until the next sound is heard. Some receivers can be programmed to adjust the delay at the end of a transmission between 2 and 10 sec.

Summary: Virtually all modern receivers have a scanning facility.

Search
The ability to search through frequencies is similar to the scanning mode referred to earlier, and the two terms are, in fact, sometimes confused.

Scanning applies only to memorised frequencies. Searching is concerned with stepping through every channel between an upper and lower limit.

Above:
Long-range radar station at Lowther Hill, Scotland.
Derek M. McCabe/Civil Aviation Authority

Some sets can only scan between the lowest frequency and the highest frequency, monitoring every channel in sequence until a transmission is heard.

More sophisticated receivers can be programmed to search between any two frequencies decided by the listener. The ability to 'delay' or to 'hold', as described earlier under the heading 'Scanning', also applies to the 'Search' mode.

There are a number of receivers on which it is possible to transfer any frequency on which transmissions are detected directly into the memory of the set — this applies both to the 'Scan' and 'Search' modes.

Summary: The ability to search is a positive advantage, but not essential. It is probably of most use to the beginner who is unsure of individual frequencies. Most modern scanners have this facility.

Pass (or Lockout)
Scanners with facilities for searching or scanning are often provided with a 'pass' function.

As the receiver will, of course, stop at any sound it detects it is often the case that some of those signals will not be wanted by the listener — for example, continuous weather transmissions, airfield information transmissions, or simply interference.

Whenever the set stops at an unwanted frequency the 'pass' key is pressed. The search (or scan) then continues, the locked-out frequencies subsequently being ignored by the receiver. Any frequency which has been locked out can be brought back into the circuit by pressing the 'pass' key again.

Summary: Lockout or pass is a feature which applies only to receivers with Scan or Search modes. Most sets with Scan/Search will be capable of lockout.

Frequency Selection

One question often overlooked concerns the simplicity of changing frequency.

It is usually possible to step through memorised frequencies manually, both forwards or backwards, or to similarly move in either direction through the entire range by manually switching from one frequency to the next.

In other cases, it may be necessary to enter every individual frequency, as required, by manual means. The frequencies selected will, of course, vary depending on the steps programmed into the receiver by the user.

Some scanners have a feature which allows frequencies to be changed forwards or backwards by means of a rotary tuning knob.

Some modern sets have a small display screen which shows the chosen frequency, plus a stand-by second frequency. Switching between the two channels is simple and rapid. It is also possible with some of the more expensive receivers to indicate the selected frequency with the title of the particular service.

Summary: A relatively minor consideration, but one which can make listening far more convenient.

Power Supply

There are several alternative methods of providing power to your airband receiver.

Batteries

These can be ordinary dry cell batteries or the rechargeable type.

Normal batteries are expensive for everyday use, especially if the receiver is used mainly as a base station in the home or in a car.

Rechargeable batteries are very economical in use, once the initial cost of purchasing the recharging unit and at least two sets of batteries has been met. (The second set of batteries is necessary so that the receiver can still be used while the first set is being recharged.)

These batteries can be recharged hundreds of times at a very low cost, although their 'life' in the receiver is quite low — perhaps a few hours — so they are not the most suitable type for sets used almost continuously.

Some receivers are provided with the means for recharging the batteries while still in the set. The recharging unit also serves as a power supply source which operates the receiver directly. The recharger, therefore, operates the scanner when it is in use, and continues to recharge the batteries when the receiver is switched off.

Again, the rechargeable batteries will only be effective for no more than a few hours, so if it is intended to use the set outside for a longer period it is preferable to use normal long-life batteries instead of rechargeables. Remember that most base station receivers are not designed to operate on batteries.

Also, some modern scanners do not operate very well on rechargeable batteries. They seem to require the high power out-put of dry cell extra long life batteries for best results.

12V Car Power

Most modern scanners are provided with a connection for an external power source and this can be used for an adapter which can be connected to the cigarette lighter socket of a vehicle. The adapter must be switched to the correct output voltage appropriate to the receiver, and it is also important to ensure that the polarity of the connections are matched to the set. Car power adapters are usually provided with a reversible polarity socket, so the 'plus' and 'minus' connection to the receiver can easily be fitted incorrectly. Care must be taken to match the connections correctly so that the set is not damaged.

Mains Operation

Similar to the car supply is the adapter operating from the mains supply. Obviously this provides the easiest and most economic method of supplying a continuously stable and reliable source of power for receivers operating from a home base.

Most of the top manufacturers of airband receivers are able to supply a mains adapter suitable for that particular product, but sometimes it will be necessary to obtain a separate adapter from an independent supplier, in which case care is needed to make sure the unit is compatible with the receiver. It is advisable to purchase such items only from reputable outlets as it is possible to damage the receiver by the use of unsuitable equipment.

Summary: Decide on which power supplies you are likely to need according to the type of use you anticipate.

Antenna Connections

Virtually all popular airband monitoring receivers are provided with an antenna which is

Above:
AOR 3000A communications receiver. *AOR*

connected to the set by a BNC-type fitting or, occasionally, a PL259 fitting.

The BNC type is neater and smaller and therefore less cumbersome for the smaller receiver, while the PL259 is a heavier unit. Most modern scanners are now provided with the BNC type of antenna connection. Both types can be used with antennas or receivers because each one can be adapted by the use of the correct fitting. Both connectors are used with coaxial cable. Suitable adapters for converting from one type of connector to another are available from most radio equipment suppliers. Both BNC and PL259 connections are available in versions which can be fitted without the use of solder.

Some base-station receivers are supplied without an antenna — the purchaser is expected to select a suitable antenna system most appropriate to the set, bearing in mind the location where it will be used, the proximity of transmitters and so on. Of course, any receiver with one of the usual connections can be fitted with more than one antenna — perhaps one for mobile use and one for use as a base station.

Summary: Choose a receiver with one of the popular kinds of antenna connection, preferably the BNC.

Squelch
The squelch control is a rotary switch which is used to eliminate background noise and interference. Without this facility reception is spoiled by 'hiss' and interference. In addition, the search and scan functions will not operate while any background noise is present. Also,

tape recording with a voice activated recorder will be difficult, if not impossible.

Although it may appear to be an obvious requirement in a modern expensive receiver, it is advisable to check specifically that the set does have a squelch facility.

Summary: Check that the set you are considering does have 'squelch'. Not all of them do!

Priority Channel
When a receiver is operating in either Scan or Search mode, it is common with most models to allocate one or more frequencies as a 'priority'.

This means that whenever the receiver is scanning a range of memorised channels, or searching through a sequence of frequencies, the priority channel will be sampled at regular intervals (usually about one or two seconds) to determine whether a transmission is taking place. If a signal is detected, the receiver will remain on the priority channel until the end of the message — it will then revert to the Search or Scan mode as appropriate.

Each listener will wish to select his or her own special interest channel — for example the emergency frequency of 121.5 (VHF) or 243.0 (UHF) which is used only very occasionally — but apart from this kind of use the priority channel is unlikely to be of special use to the airband listener and, in any case, such attributes do not enhance the performance of the receiver.

Summary: Priority channels can be useful but are not essential.

Inexpensive Receivers
Many people who are starting out in the field of airband listening are understandably hesitant about spending perhaps £200 on a receiver when they are unsure about the quality of the messages they are likely to receive in their area. Also, being a new hobby, they will wish to 'test the water' before reaching a decision on whether to move up-market into the realms of the sophisticated sets described earlier.

Apart from the fact that modern expensive receivers are often difficult for the beginner to master, there is also the consideration that the newcomer will almost certainly be unaware of the aeronautical activity in the area, therefore the probability of being able to get the best results is unlikely.

A possible solution in such situations is the low-price receiver (probably no more than £75 at 1999 prices) which will at least enable the listener to hear some of the VHF transmissions in the area.

The method of tuning such receivers is 'continuous' (that is, the same as an old-fashioned domestic radio receiver which operates by simply shifting a pointer across a waveband dial) so that the full range of VHF frequencies can be covered very quickly, backwards and forwards, until a transmission is detected.

Whenever a pilot or controller is heard, it is well worth noting the position on the dial by using a strip of adhesive paper across the top of the scale, suitably marked as each of the frequencies come through.

In practice, due to the design of the receiver, it is inevitable that more than one individual frequency will be heard at each position on the scale, since this kind of set is not able to separate each frequency individually.

Because of the receive's simple design the overlapping of frequencies can mean that 20 or more channels are covered by one position on the dial, resulting in a considerable spread of transmissions being received instead of a single one being detected as on the more sophisticated set.

Inexpensive receivers tend to suffer badly from local interference, with unwanted signals breaking through and obliterating aeronautical transmissions. Police messages and other similar agencies can often be heard, as well as other incomprehensible blasts of static.

One of the best ways to become an owner of an airband receiver is to consider a secondhand purchase through the advertising columns of the radio enthusiasts' magazines, or from one of the country's main radio stockists.

Both sources are ideal for the first-timer provided the purchaser asks sensible questions first concerning frequencies, frequency steps and so on, as described earlier.

Below:
Radio transmitters near Heathrow Airport. *Author*

5 Antennas

All airband scanners can be improved by the use of a dedicated external antenna system, often resulting in quite dramatic results, depending on the location of the receiver and the proximity of ATC transmitters.

Even if you are in an area where good reception is the norm, significant improvements in hearing more distant traffic will make the small investment worth while.

It does not make sense to spend a large sum of money on a scanner while ignoring the benefits of an external aerial system which can usually be provided for a fraction of the cost of the receiver.

Basic airband antennas are actually quite simple in design and well within the capabilities of the average DIY person. However, remember that the same comments apply to antennas as to receivers — spending more and more money on the antenna often has no significant effect on performance. The best all round results can be achieved with the simplest home-made systems made up from discarded television or radio aerials at virtually no expense.

Remember that VHF and UHF transmissions are generally 'line-of-sight', similar to television and FM radio. The most expensive receiver used in a location where there is no line-of-sight to the transmitter will give poor results, even with the best antenna. Alternatively, a basic low-price receiver, located in a suitable position close to a transmitter, can perform well even with the simplest aerial.

There are a few basic points to bear in mind as far as antenna 'systems' are concerned — a system being the overall design and location of the antenna, its installation, the feed to the receiver, the various connections, amplifiers and, of course, the receiver itself.

First, there are two kinds of antenna — one which is capable of receiving signals from every direction in equal strength, known as 'omni-directional', and the other which is designed to concentrate the received signals, and amplify them, from one particular point, (probably an en-route transmitter or an airport) so that the strongest possible signal is heard, in the same way that television signals are received. These are known as 'directional' aerials.

In areas of good overall airband coverage, with ATC transmitters relatively nearby and with the receiver in a good location, the omni-

Below:
In the future, HF radio could be replaced by High Frequency Datalink ground stations, each with a range of up to 5,000km for ATC and flight management. *Irish Aviation Authority*

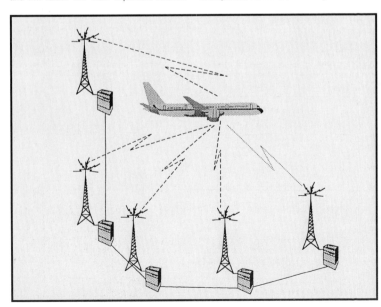

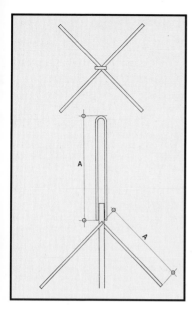

Above:
Basic ground plane antenna. The dimensions are the same as those for the simple dipole antenna.

local circumstances and the relative positions of aircraft, airfields, transmitters and other features likely to affect reception.

Antenna Design
The various types of antenna fall into two basic designs:
■ Single element vertical designs, often referred to as Marconi-type aerials, or
■ Dipoles, consisting of two separate halves of a vertical aerial which act together as a single antenna.

Marconi Antennas
The single vertical antenna is designed to operate at a particular frequency according to the length of the element. The length is arrived at by calculating the dimension of the element according to a simple formula: divide 75 by the appropriate frequency in megahertz. This gives the length of the antenna in millimetres, although for best results 5% of the length should be deducted.

The frequencies used for aeronautical communication range between 118MHz at the lowest end, on VHF, to 400MHz at the highest,

Below:
A simple but effective dipole antenna consisting of two vertical elements separated by insulated material.

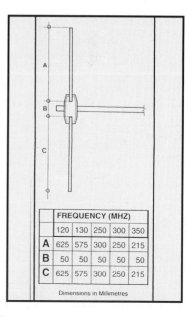

FREQUENCY (MHZ)					
	120	130	250	300	350
A	625	575	300	250	215
B	50	50	50	50	50
C	625	575	300	250	215

Dimensions in Millimetres

directional system will perform quite adequately. Other locations, surrounded by high ground, massive buildings or simply remote from airports or transmitter stations, may well benefit from a directional type of antenna which can at least be pointed towards an airport, or an en-route transmitter, so as to obtain the best possible signal even though it may be less than perfect.

Whether you decide upon an omni-directional antenna or one which is directional will, of course, depend upon your particular listening base and your individual requirements.

If you are listening in an area which is generally poor, in reception terms, then you may well consider an antenna which can be pointed towards an en-route transmitter, or an airport, so that any available signals can be detected at the best possible level. The locations of ATC transmitters across the UK are given in the chart.

The disadvantage with a directional system is the fact that signals from other sources (aircraft, for example) may be heard at a much reduced level.

It is impossible to give positive advice for every situation since so much depends upon the

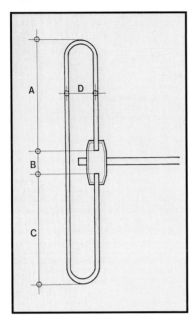

Above:
A variation of the simple dipole — the folded dipole. The dimensions are the same as those for the simple dipole.

Ground Plane Antennas

The single element antenna may operate more effectively if it is provided with a system of radials (usually four) at its base (known as a ground screen). An antenna of this design, with a vertical element and radials, is known as a 'ground plane'. However, an improvement in reception over the basic design cannot be guaranteed.

Each of the radials should be cut to the same length as the vertical element and angled downwards at approximately 45° to give the best results.

The centre core of the coaxial cable should be connected to the vertical element, with the outer braid connected to the ground plane elements. The vertical element and the ground screen must be insulated from each other.

Dipoles

Perhaps the most popular 'do-it-yourself' antenna is the dipole. This consists of two single elements (as described earlier) mounted vertically, one above the other, with the centre core of the coaxial cable connected to the upper element and the outer braid connected to the lower element. Again, it is essential that the antenna is constructed in such a way that the two elements are insulated from each other. This can be achieved by fixing the elements to a base board of rigid plastic, for example, or by the use of a suitable cable connector box which can be purchased from shops dealing with television and radio aerials. A suitable aerial can be made from an FM radio antenna with the two elements shortened to the correct dimensions.

Each of the two elements should be cut to the length which is appropriate to the chosen frequency, using the formula given earlier. The overall length of the antenna is therefore twice that of the single element type.

If it is required to have an aerial system suitable for listening to both VHF and UHF transmissions, two Marconi-type antennas, or alternatively two dipole antennas, can be erected side by side in a location as high as possible, with separate coaxial down-leads to the receiver. The two antennas must be cut to length for the respective UHF and VHF frequencies, and the leads will have to be switched from one antenna to the other according to the station being received.

It is, of course, quite feasible to use one single antenna, of either design, cut to an average length midway between the two optimum dimensions suggested for VHF and UHF — say 425mm. This will give an acceptable performance and may well be suitable if the location of the receiver is reasonably close to transmitter sites. Obviously, an 'average' design can never be as good as one prepared specifically for a narrow range of frequencies,

on UHF. By using the formula for single element vertical antennas the lengths vary from 603mm to 178mm (75 divided by 118 and 75 divided by 400 respectively, less 5%)

Obviously, as it is not practical to design the antenna for these two extreme frequencies, it is more sensible to choose an average rating appropriate to the most popular frequency in your area.

When deciding upon the antenna length, unless there is a specific frequency of particular interest, a mid-range average can be used, probably around 127MHz for VHF (giving a dimension of around 600mm) and perhaps 300MHz for UHF (resulting in a dimension of approximately 250mm).

For most purposes an antenna suitable for the middle of the range of frequencies will usually be adequate.

Do not worry too much about being accurate about the exact measurements. The final result will be influenced to a far greater extent by other factors (such as the height of the antenna, good clean connections and so on) so the dimensions should be looked upon as no more than a guide.

so the decision as to how the problem is tackled is one for each individual listener according to the circumstances. There is no doubt that a dedicated design for a specific frequency will give the best results.

Do not be misled into assuming that because these simple antennas are relatively easy and cheap to make that they are less effective than other antennas advertised and sold by specialist companies. Experience shows that they are very efficient and can be just as good as those which can be purchased ready made. In fact, some airband listeners maintain that their home-made antennas actually give a performance which is better than the professional models. These simple designs have been shown to out-perform many of the so-called high-tech models.

Below:
A directional antenna constructed in accordance with these dimensions may be used in areas of poor reception.

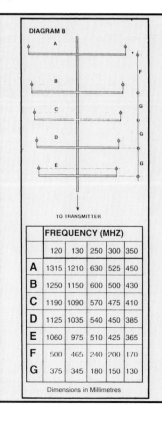

| DIAGRAM 8 |
| TO TRANSMITTER |

FREQUENCY (MHZ)					
	120	130	250	300	350
A	1315	1210	630	525	450
B	1250	1150	600	500	430
C	1190	1090	570	475	410
D	1125	1035	540	450	385
E	1060	975	510	425	365
F	500	465	240	200	170
G	375	345	180	150	130

Dimensions in Millimetres

Folded Dipoles

A marginally more efficient version of the dipole antenna is the type known as a 'folded' dipole in which a normal dipole design is provided with an additional element which connects the two extreme ends, resulting in an antenna with slightly improved capabilities when compared to the normal dipole. The dimensions of the two arms are calculated by using the same formula as given previously. Often, however, the improvement is negligible and not worth the effort.

Nests of Dipoles

For complete coverage of a wide range of frequencies capable of handling VHF and UHF, it is possible to link together a series of dipole aerials of different lengths, cut according to the frequencies required and fed to the receiver with a single coaxial lead.

This kind of antenna has become known as a 'nest of dipoles'. They are available commercially but it is also possible to make one at home for internal use and reports as to its effectiveness are very favourable.

If it is desired to listen only to one range of frequencies (VHF airband, for example) it will probably not be worth the time and expense to provide a multiple dipole type of antenna, since the range of frequencies is relatively short and reception is unlikely to be greatly improved by such a system. A straightforward dipole will almost certainly be adequate.

Directional Antennas

All the systems discussed so far are types which operate on an 'omni-directional' principle. In other words, the signals detected by these antennas are received in more or less equal strength from every direction. This is usually ideal for the average airband listener.

Aircraft transmissions invariably come from all directions and it can be counter-productive to think of concentrating the signals into one direction because those from other areas may be lost or seriously impaired.

But there may be situations where there will be a benefit from 'aiming' the antenna towards a particular location, either a remote ATC transmitter or an airfield, so as to amplify the transmission which might otherwise go unheard.

These antennas are again based on a dipole design, but instead of being fixed vertically, they are placed horizontally with the signals being concentrated by separate elements placed behind and in front of the main dipole.

This design of aerial is known as a 'Yagi- type antenna.

The dimensions of the dipole part of the antenna are arrived at by the same calculation as for the more usual omni-directional types referred to earlier. The other elements and their distances apart are calculated in accordance with the diagrams. Although these may appear rather complex, they are actually quite easy to make from aluminium tube, but if your skills in the DIY line are limited one of the local television aerial companies might be persuaded to make up a design to suit your requirements.

Another way to manufacture a directional antenna for positioning in a loft is to attach copper wire or fine tubing to a lightweight flat polystyrene sheet (obtainable from builders merchants) following the design measurements. This can be located in a convenient position and is easier to assemble than a traditional design. The completed article is then placed in a suitable position in the roof space, directed towards the source of the signals.

Mobile Antennas

Most airband listeners will want to spend at least some of their time listening to aircraft at airports or in other areas away from their home base. Often the built-in aerial will be adequate, but performance will undoubtedly be improved with a separate external antenna. The most popular type is a single element aerial with a magnetic base which is attached to the roof of a vehicle, the metal roof acting as a ground screen.

Another type of portable aerial consists of a length of ribbon antenna with a cable connection for the receiver. This can be used in any location, but is particularly useful since it can be folded away and easily manufacture. It is impractical to attempt to manufacture such antennas as DIY projects; they are not too expensive to buy and are readily available from the suppliers quoted at the end of the book.

Active Antenna Systems

An active antenna is one which uses electrical power for its operation. It is often much smaller than a conventional antenna and can therefore be used in smaller spaces. The power supply is provided from a battery or through a transformer from the mains. Active antennas are particularly useful in areas of poor reception and where the use of an external antenna is not possible.

Unfortunately, it is very difficult to assess the efficiency of each design without having direct experience in your particular location. Sometimes the results will be good but at other times they may be disappointing.

It may be possible to persuade your supplier to agree to refund the cost if the antenna is unsuitable.

Cables

The cable used with antennas suitable for UHF and VHF aeronautical transmissions is a coaxial type, very similar to television cable. It consists of a central core surrounded by insulation and covered by a woven wire screen which is then surrounded by a plastic outer cover.

Although television cable may provide acceptable results in some situations, it is more appropriate to use a cable of the 'low loss' type since these provide the best performance with the lowest degree of signal loss.

The cables normally specified for airband use are known as UR43 or UR67, both available from airband radio companies or the specialist cable suppliers. These cables are designed to fit the BNC-type fitting used on most of today's scanners.

Using these cables may not result in any significant advantage over television cable, but it is probably worth using the best quality product for the relatively small extra outlay involved. If your receiver is in a poor location, it is certainly good sense to use the very best low loss cable available.

Connections

Most modern receivers have antenna connections which are likely to be one of two types, known as PL259 or BNC.

In recent years the BNC connection has become more popular; it is compact, easy to connect and efficient. The PL259 is heavy and more cumbersome, although equally effective. Both types can be obtained in solderless versions, making them easy to fit. Whichever type is fitted to your receiver, there are adaptors which convert BNC to PL259 and vice versa so

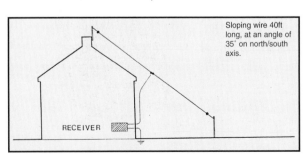

Sloping wire 40ft long, at an angle of 35° on north/south axis.

Left:
In restricted areas, this long wire HF antenna can be used.

RECEIVER

there should be no problem with either fitting.

Some receivers, particularly in the low price range, may have one of several other kinds of antenna connection, but these are relatively unusual and it can be assumed that the majority of popular sets will be fitted with BNC or PL259 connections.

Low-priced receivers are probably fitted with simple extending aerials, often fixed to the receiver so that it is not possible to fit external antennas directly to the receiver. If it is intended to connect a separate aerial the simplest method is to fully close the receiver's aerial and connect the external antenna to it by means of a small crocodile clip fed from the centre core of the coaxial cable.

Cable Feed

When deciding upon a suitable route for the antenna cable it is necessary to consider whether the cable will be placed close to anything which is likely to interfere with the quality of the reception.

The cable run should be as short as reasonably practical but, more importantly, it should avoid any items of electrical equipment, especially television receivers and fluorescent light fittings. It also needs to be as close to vertical as possible for best results. The antenna itself can be hung in the loft (tape a piece of strong string to the top of the antenna and hang it from the ridge timber in the roof space).

However, better results will usually be obtained if the antenna is fitted externally, away from other objects.

Antenna Manufacturers

Many of the antennas on sale today are not designed specifically for the airband listeners' market — instead the antennas are suitable for wide coverage, not only for VHF and UHF aeronautical messages, but also for other kinds of transmissions, therefore the quality of reception is the result of a compromise in design. Wide-band designs are not usually as efficient for airband listening as those specifically designed for the purpose.

If your main interest is airband, then certainly try a simple home-made approach first — if this does not work, by all means experiment with more sophisticated commercial systems in an attempt to improve matters, but do not be surprised if the results are not what was expected.

Summary

Whether you decide to choose a separate antenna to help your listening pleasure or alternatively simply stay with the aerial provided with the receiver is a matter of choice. Many factors will influence your decision, the most important being related to the proximity of the various transmitting stations in your area.

If you do most of your listening near large busy airfields or close to en-route transmitter sites, the simple antenna system might well be sufficient for good quality listening. Unfortunately, most of us are not in such a fortunate position. Living in relatively remote areas (in ATC terms) or surrounded by high ground and large buildings means that an efficient external antenna is essential.

In any case, no matter how good the quality, without a sophisticated antenna in areas of good reception there is little doubt that an external antenna will improve the range of messages received.

One final point to bear in mind is that many hand-held scanners can be overloaded by strong signals received through an external antenna. Base station sets are designed to operate with high gain aerials and there should be little difficulty in obtaining reasonable results. Depending on your location, an external system may be disappointing if it is connected to a lightweight hand-held receiver.

Below:
'SCANAP' air band receiver. *Waters & Stanton*

6 High Frequency Radio

Previous chapters have covered VHF and UHF aeronautical radio, both of which are very effective when the transmitter and the receiver are fairly close to each other — in the region of 200 miles or so. The line-of-sight principle applies to all aircraft communications in densely populated areas of the world. However, when flights are crossing large uninhabited regions or the oceans it is necessary to employ another system of communication.

The method in use today is the High Frequency (or Short Wave) radio coverage which operates over long distances. It is the only suitable method at the present time of maintaining contact with flights which are crossing remote areas such as the Atlantic, the Pacific, the Indian Ocean and Africa.

The nearest area to the UK which has HF radio as its primary means of contact is the North Atlantic; in excess of 1,000 flights are being handled on a busy day in midsummer.

Atlantic flights are first required to file a flight plan which must include the airways across the land areas, together with the point of entry into the ocean region and the proposed route (or 'track') together with the aircraft's requested flight level and speed.

Once beyond the range of land based radars and radio transmitters on VHF and UHF the ATC service will change from a radar control situation to one where the safety of the flight depends on reports passed by long-range radio back to the control centre, perhaps 2,000 miles distant.

Position reports are made in a predetermined format at set intervals to radio receiving stations where the operators pass the details of the aircraft's location to the appropriate control centre for comparison with the flight plan. This all takes place without the benefit of radar; separation of aircraft depends upon accurate radio reports from the flight crews and the actual location of the flight depends, in turn, on the accuracy of the navigation capabilities of the aircraft and the skill of the flight crew.

The only communication system which is suitable for these long range transmissions is High Frequency' radio or, more usually, 'HF'. Until a few years ago the term used was 'Short Wave' radio but this description has generally been superseded, although both terms ('HF' and 'Short Wave') have the same meaning.

High Frequency transmissions for aeronautical use take place between 2MHz and 23MHz, in certain specific groups. Each group of frequencies is referred to as a 'family'.

The reason for such a wide selection of cover on the HF bands is due to the peculiar characteristics of the behaviour of transmissions across the range. Long range radio is affected to a great extent by atmospheric conditions and by the effect of daylight and darkness on the quality of the signal.

Because of the curvature of the earth, it is not possible for an aircraft to receive transmissions from a distant ground based transmitter, on VHF or UHF since the two stations will be out of sight of each other. Occasionally freak conditions exist which do make long distance reception possible, but the times during which this is possible are so rare as to be impractical for regular use.

High Frequency transmissions, however, between are able to travel across long distances because the signal from the transmitter travels upwards at an angle and is then reflected back down again at a similar angle so that it is possible for the message to be detected by the ground receiver or by an aircraft in flight.

The conditions (known as 'propagation') which exist at the time of the transmission have a dramatic effect on the resulting quality of reception, and it is not always easy to predict how good the performance will be at any particular time.

Each agency operating on the HF bands will have been allocated a family of frequencies, which are roughly spread across the aeronautical range between 2 and 23MHz. This enables the operator to choose any one of the frequencies in order to obtain the most effective result. As a general rule, frequencies at the lower end of the scale will be found to be more efficient during periods when both the transmitter and the receiver are in darkness, while frequencies at the high end of the range will usually be best when both receiving and transmitting stations are in full daylight. Forecasts of the likely propagation for HF transmissions are published by the aviation authorities covering the various times of the year and the hours of daylight and darkness.

For the North Atlantic, the families of frequencies are in the ranges 2, 5, 8, 11 and 17MHz.

At any one time, the frequency which has been found to give the best service in terms of loudness and clarity will be referred to as the 'primary' frequency, with a second choice backup frequency, in another part of the range, known as the 'secondary' frequency.

Listeners to HF radio will find that the reception of transmission can be predicted to a reasonably certain extent and experienced users will be able to judge quite accurately which of the frequencies to listen to at any particular time.

Above:
Airbus A330. *Airbus Industrie*

Unfortunately, one of the problems with HF radio is the fact that so many frequencies are available for use that the possibility of hearing traffic on any particular one is lower than with VHF or UHF radio.

The signals which travel upwards, and then downwards to earth, will to a greater or lesser degree continue to 'skip' across the surface of the earth until they reach right round the globe in favourable situations. On the other hand, interference on HF radio is often a problem, sometimes spoiling reception to such an extent that the messages are unreadable.

Many listeners to aeronautical radio are fascinated by HF radio. Whereas VHF or UHF messages are reasonably predictable and of fairly consistent quality, this cannot really be said of HF transmissions. There is also a wider variety of messages, especially of a 'company' nature, where pilots call their operating base with requests or reports on all kinds of matters.

Because the line-of-sight principle is not a matter of concern with HF, there is also a positive advantage for those people who are in areas of the country which are restricted in their ability to hear VHF or UHF transmissions due to the limitations of the surrounding terrain.

There are several parts of the UK where the number of transmissions on VHF or UHF are few and far between. Probably the only messages heard will be those from high flying en-route traffic which is virtually overhead, so the satisfaction level for the enthusiast will be very low. With HF radio, the situation is completely different. Someone in the middle of the Lake District, for example, can listen to New York Oceanic Control Centre in contact with flights in their area of control with as much ease as anyone else.

Apart from the differences related to the kind of reception which can be expected, the messages themselves are quite different from those heard on VHF or UHF.

One of the main differences is that the aircraft on HF radio are not normally handled by Air Traffic Control, but by radio operators who relay their messages between pilots and the control centre. In the main, the messages are related to position reports from pilots, or clearances to climb, descend, follow a particular route or change speed.

Other frequently heard messages are between pilots and their bases ('company' messages) often via agency stations which pass on details or alternatively connect the pilots with their company via the telephone network — a procedure known as 'patching'.

The agencies are often quite remote from the caller and the station being contacted. It is not unusual for a pilot on the ground in Geneva (for example) to contact Berne Radio (in Switzerland) and then to be 'patched' through to Shannon, perhaps, with their message. The pilot in Geneva will then talk directly to his contact in Shannon and their discussion can normally be heard in the UK without very much difficulty.

Shanwick Radio

The Oceanic Area which creates the most interest in the UK and Europe is the North Atlantic Oceanic Region, known as 'NARTEL' — the North Atlantic Radio Telephony Network, which covers the regions of Shanwick, Gander, Santa Maria, New York and Iceland.

The HF radio station is at Ballygirreen near Shannon, and it is from this location that messages are sent to aircraft over the North Atlantic in the Shanwick Oceanic Region.

As flights cross Europe and the United Kingdom towards the North Atlantic and Canada, they reach the oceanic 'entry points' for the Atlantic crossing. The crew will then be instructed to contact Shanwick Oceanic Control Centre at Prestwick (in Scotland) on the appropriate HF frequency, which in fact will be done via the radio station at Ballygirreen.

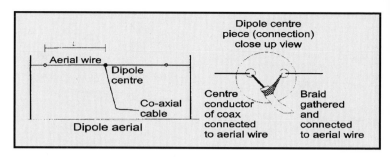

Dipole centre piece (connection) close up view

Aerial wire

Dipole centre

Co-axial cable

Dipole aerial

Centre conductor of coax connected to aerial wire

Braid gathered and connected to aerial wire

Above:
Typical long-wire dipole antenna for HF listening.
AOR Ltd

As the flight continues across the North Atlantic position reports will be made, at approximately hourly intervals, on HF frequencies.

Each transmission will be made on the primary or secondary frequency which will be heard not only at Shanwick (Ballygirreen) but also by the other North Atlantic stations at Gander, Santa Maria and New York.

All the radio stations in the NARTEL region are able to talk between themselves on the same frequencies that the flights use — in fact they can often be heard checking flight details of individual aircraft with each other.

Other areas of the world, of course, are covered by other control centres on different radio frequencies, details of which are given in the diagrams and the appendices.

HF Radio Receivers

If you wish to listen to aircraft messages on HF you need to obtain a radio receiver of a particular type, although you will find that they are more expensive than models suitable for VHF or UHF. If cost is a consideration, the airband listener will have to decide whether the extra expense is justified, especially bearing in mind that during the next ten years or so HF aeronautical communications will be phased out in favour of satellite coverage of the main areas of the world.

None of the HF radio receivers are exclusively for airband use, so they will still be suitable for listening to the many other interesting transmissions which take place.

There are far fewer HF radios available compared with VHF; it is also particularly important to appreciate the requirements necessary in an HF set which is to be used for aeronautical purposes. There is an increasing tendency for manufacturers to provide scanners which cover the entire aeronautical range of frequencies within the design of hand-held receivers. VHF and UHF are transmitted on AM whereas HF is transmitted on Upper Side Band, part of the single side band range. All of these facilities are now available in small portable

receivers, although they cannot be expected to perform as well as dedicated shortwave receivers.

Aviation agencies transmit on the Single Side Band (SSB) system, which means that more channels can be accommodated within the same space and also that less interference occurs. Equipment with SSB is further divided into two alternatives: Upper Side Band or Lower Side Band. For our purposes the receiver has to be suitable for operating on Upper Side Band, otherwise it will not be capable of resolving aircraft messages.

For airband use, an HF radio receiver must be capable of the following:

■ the frequencies are to be within the range of 2MHz to 23MHz without any breaks in the coverage;
■ Single Side Band must be provided; also the transmissions must be capable of operating on Upper Side Band;
■ digital entry of the precise frequency is desirable.

Some of the lower priced receivers have a tuning system whereby the main frequency is selected, and the precise frequency is found by a sensitive tuning dial known as a Beat Frequency Oscillator which must be used to finely tune the receiver. In fact, this is a relatively slow process and requires practice. For aeronautical purposes the signal is often finished before it can be tuned accurately. Good quality receivers will be more expensive than those for VHF and UHF.

As there are so many frequencies in use for aviation purposes, the ability to add them to the receiver's memory is a considerable advantage, but none of the currently available sets has a total of memories greater than a few dozen.

Short Wave Antennas

It is normally quite easy to receive airband messages on VHF or UHF, since reception depends on line-of-sight between the transmitter and the receiver. Provided the signal is not interrupted by large obstructions such as large buildings or hills, reception will probably be reasonably good at ranges up to 50 miles for ground transmitters or 200 miles for aircraft in flight.

With High Frequency radio the reception is far less predictable even though the antenna system may be far from sophisticated. Often a simple length of wire connected to the receiver will give results which are as good as any more expensive system.

The quality of reception on HF depends so much on changing atmospheric conditions that the aerial system may not have a significant effect on the final result. However, it is perhaps worth trying some of the variations because one particular type might just work well in your circumstances. Unfortunately, no one particular type can be said to be better or worse than any other. It is very much a case of experimenting with the various options before a final decision is made, but even then it is quite possible that the simplest design is likely to be the most efficient.

Antenna Systems

Most types of antenna suitable for use on HF are basically simple, consisting in the main of long lengths of wire stretched out in the open, in a roof space or around a room. If used out of doors a multi-strand pvc-covered wire specially made for such use is recommended because it can stand the strain of being pulled in tension between two points over a considerable distance.

There are a number of main kinds of HF antenna and these are described below.

Long Wire

This type of antenna is one of the simplest to install and yet still one of the most effective for HF listening. The wire should be not less than 30ft, stretched out in the open as high as reasonably possible, usually between the house and a pole or a tree, and insulated at each end by ceramic or plastic insulators which can be obtained from specialist suppliers.

The wire has to be strong enough to support itself and it must also be capable of resisting any corrosion. A long length of wire of perhaps 50ft needs a considerable load to stretch it to the horizontal position, therefore only the correct kind of wire is suitable.

Theoretically a 'north-south' installation will give the best results for traffic on the North Atlantic, although in practice this cannot be achieved in many cases. Other factors such as the proximity of buildings or hills may well affect the efficiency of the antenna so that adequate results can be obtained.

The end of the wire closest to the receiver should be run down to the receiver, as near to vertical as possible, and then to the external antenna socket on the receiver. If it is unavoidable to route the cable through the building, care must be taken to avoid any electrical circuits or television receivers.

Dipole Antenna

This is a variation on the simple long-wire type of antenna. The wire is also stretched outside, in the clear, preferably at least 30ft in length and insulated at both ends in the same way as the long wire type. The difference is that the centre of the wire is cut and joined via a suitable weatherproof connection box to a coaxial down-lead (eg UR67) with the centre core being connected to one arm of the dipole and the outer braid to the outer arm. The other end of the UR67 cable is connected to the receiver with the appropriate connector plug.

In order to ensure that the two arms of the dipole are matched, the junction at the point of the break in the main wire can be made by using a 'balun' transformer which balances the signal received so that (in theory at least) an improved signal will be received at the receiver. Again, it may well be necessary to experiment with such systems so that their suitability can be assessed. Many companies offer variations of wire antennas and components for HF use.

Sloping Dipole Antenna

If space is a problem it might not be possible to erect a long wire type of antenna, therefore some kind of alternative system has to be considered. In confined gardens the only suitable option could be to provide a system which achieves the required length but without taking up too much space. In this design the wire is sloped at an angle so that the proportions are roughly equivalent to a 3:4:5 triangle, ie 30ft/40ft/50ft with the 50ft arm being the actual antenna.

To get the dimensions right it will be necessary to fit the highest end of the antenna wire to a mast on the chimney stack or to the highest point of a gable roof. Fixing the wire at the fascia level of the average two-storey house will not usually be high enough to achieve the correct proportions.

The connection to the receiver is made in the same way as for the previous dipole design, by splitting the wire at the centre and connecting a coaxial cable to the two elements.

Indoor Aerials

There will always be situations where it is not possible or convenient for an external antenna to be fitted, for example in flats.

In these cases the provision of an indoor antenna can often be quite acceptable and because the wire will not have to resist the weather or support its own weight it will be satisfactory to use thin wire which can be fitted in the roof space, around the room, under the carpet or even behind the wallpaper. The object in all cases is to provide at least 30ft of continuous wire stretched out as far as possible, although not necessarily in a straight line.

If possible, two independent antennas positioned at right angles to each other will be well worth considering since each can be tried in different conditions in order to obtain the best results.

To avoid interference, the antenna wires should be kept away from electrical circuits, television receivers and other electrical fittings.

Active Antennas
This term is used to describe a type of antenna which is electrically powered, the electronics being designed to match the signal at the receiver to the aerial. The antenna itself will be three or four feet in length, and is therefore suitable for fixing almost anywhere which is convenient. It is powered either by a mains transformer or by batteries, and although it may not be particularly better than a long wire design, it should give adequate results and is ideal where space is a problem or where a quick and simple system is desired.

Earthing
It is important that any HF aerial system should be isolated from the receiver to prevent damage in the event of a lightning strike. It is also recommended that a separate earth be taken from the set to a length of copper tube or rod driven into the soil to give improved reception.

Lightning Protection
Most suppliers recommend a suitable means of isolating the antenna system from the receiver so that in the event of a lightning strike the receiver will not be damaged. An arrester provided between the antenna and the set will prevent lightning damage, although it is not very likely in this part of the world.

The necessary equipment can be purchased from radio equipment suppliers and fitted in accordance with the manufacturer's recommendations.

If for any reason you are using your receiver without such protection then it is advisable to disconnect the antenna lead from the equipment when not in use or whenever there is a possibility of an electrical storm.

Aerial Tuning Units (ATUs)
It is worth experimenting with an Aerial Tuning Unit (ATU) when using a long wire type of antenna. The

Above:
Locations of ATC radio transmitters in the UK.

ATU adjusts the signal on any particular frequency to match the length of the antenna wire so that the best results are obtained.

As the ATU is adjusted the signal can be heard to improve as the background interference is reduced.

It is not necessary to spend a large sum on an ATU — simple inexpensive models usually give acceptable results.

Conclusion
The reception of transmissions on HF is not very predictable. Changes occur within a matter of a few hours, resulting in dramatic effects on the quality of reception. Sometimes the simplest of aerials, perhaps the in-built telescopic type, can give very good results; at other times reception is poor despite the most expensive and elaborate system. It is often a good idea to have two different systems in operation. Switching from one to the other so that the best results are achieved is usually worth while.

Although HF radio is still the main means of communication in remote areas, the use of datalinking is increasing, especially in the area of company messages. Datalink is more reliable and much faster than radio, and already North Atlantic track clearances are sent to many of the world's major airlines by this method. Within a few years flight plan clearances to aircraft at airports will also be using this system, and as satellites become more reliable there is little doubt that the use of HF will diminish.

7 Towards Better Listening

An understanding of some of the processes involved in ATC transmissions will help the listener to obtain improved results from a scanner. The first section covers the occasional use of two frequencies at the same time.

Simultaneous Transmissions

At quiet periods, when traffic is light, adjacent sectors will be operated together. The two frequencies will be used at the same time, a system known as 'band-boxing'.

These almost always occur at times of the day when traffic levels are low and controller workload reduced; usually this is very early in the morning or late in the evening.

At these relatively quiet periods there is no need to keep the normal daytime number of controllers handling flights; the control centres will therefore close down some of their sector positions and transfer the control of aircraft in those sectors to adjacent controllers. In itself this is straightforward enough; the complication for the airband listener is that although there is one controller handling traffic in two sectors, the controller will often use two frequencies simultaneously. The listener will hear the controller talking to aircraft in both sectors but will hear replies only from aircraft in one of the sectors — the one to which the scanner is tuned.

Imagine two adjacent sectors — Sector A and Sector B. (Sectors are air traffic control areas for en-route flights.) Sector A operates on VHF frequency 134.5, Sector B on 126.5. During normal operations, traffic in each sector would be handled by two separate control teams. As the traffic levels reduce, Sector B controller will hand over control of the traffic in the sector to the Sector A controller. Section A controller will then handle all the flights in both sectors. Flights in Sector A will transmit on 134.5, flights in Sector B will transmit on 126.5. The controller will talk to flights in both sectors, using both frequencies simultaneously. If your receiver is tuned to 134.5 you will hear all the controller's messages, on both frequencies, but only the replies from traffic in Sector A.

If the period of reduced traffic load is likely to be prolonged, the aircraft in both sectors will be transferred to one of the two frequencies. Both controllers and flights will then be on one frequency, until traffic increases and the requirement for two sector controllers becomes necessary.

Another occasional change from normal routine needs some explanation. In the example described earlier it sometimes happens that the aircraft appear to be transmitting on both sector frequencies, while the controller's messages are also heard on both frequencies.

In fact, the aircraft radio is not capable of being used on two frequencies simultaneously. Aircraft transmit on one frequency (the appropriate sector frequency). The message is picked up at one of the ATC radio receiving stations, and this is then instantly retransmitted on a different frequency for the other sector.

If you have access to two receivers you can verify this by tuning them to the two sector frequencies — you will hear identical transmissions from aircraft on the two sets simultaneously. However, this does not happen very often so it may never be heard in your area.

Aircraft messages being retransmitted in this way can mean a dramatic improvement in the quality of reception. An aircraft perhaps 250 miles away can transmit to a receiving station possibly only 50 miles away. The retransmitted message is then heard at full strength from a much closer location, giving the impression that the flight is nearer than it really is. There are other reasons for dramatic improvements in the range and quality of ATC transmissions, mainly due to the weather. These are discussed later.

Offset Frequencies

Several airband scanners are provided with the facility for selecting a variety of frequency steps, some as small as 0.1kHz.

The current steps between published frequencies in the airband range are 25kHz for VHF and UHF transmissions. Some receivers cannot be adjusted to receive frequencies other than those published.

In practice, however, many en-route transmissions are made on frequencies which are in fact slightly higher or slightly lower than those published, and these are known as 'offsets'. In the UK, these are plus or minus 2.5, 5 or 7.5kHz.

In order to obtain maximum range the ground transmissions for en-route traffic are made simultaneously from two, three or four separate transmitters; to avoid interference between the transmitters, the actual frequencies used are slightly higher or lower than those published.

Radio receivers fitted in aircraft are designed to cope with these variations in frequency; similarly anyone listening to a particular frequency with an airband receiver will have no reception difficulties provided one of the transmitters is nearby, as the strength of the signal will not create any problem.

On the fringe of cover it is a different matter. The fact that the transmission is taking place on a slightly different frequency can result in the loss of the signal altogether; airband listeners are often in locations where ground control transmissions are difficult or impossible to receive. If the receiver is tuned to the published frequency this may in fact result in you being unable to hear the messages. Having an airband scanner with the facility of selecting small frequency steps can be a distinct advantage. Several modern receivers are tunable in 1kHz steps or less, so that the actual frequency chosen can be higher or lower than the one published. It is often the case that one of these frequencies will give better results. In situations where reception is difficult, one of the offset frequencies will enable the controller to be heard even though this may not be possible on the original frequency.

Offsets do not apply to airfield situations. The modern development of providing airband receivers with the ability to select steps as low as 0.1kHz gives the listener a complete range of frequencies to choose from.

Effect of Weather
Occasionally, in the spring or autumn, the weather system will provide conditions which give exceptional results in VHF and UHF reception. Such opportunities are quite rare — perhaps half a dozen times a year — but it is usually quite easy to predict when these conditions are likely to occur.

The most common situation for improved reception is a combination of fog and a high pressure system covering the country, probably occurring during the early morning and lasting perhaps until lunchtime.

Reception of controllers' messages from transmitters perhaps 200 miles away are likely to be received without difficulty, plus other broadcasts which might not usually be heard — for example, Volmet, Oceanic Track Clearances and even airport controllers over 100 miles away.

Generally a weather forecast of widespread fog during the spring or autumn will indicate that ATC transmissions will be dramatically improved.

As the fog lifts, and the weather gradually improves, the rarely heard transmissions will slowly diminish in quality, with the background noise becoming worse until eventually the signal will be lost altogether.

Attenuators
The dictionary definition of 'attenuate' is to reduce in force or value. This is precisely the effect of an attenuator fitted between a radio receiver and the antenna — the signal reaching the set is reduced in strength, the level varying according to the value of the attenuator.

Attenuators are normally used to cancel out unwanted signals — naturally, if the transmissions are being received loudly and

clearly there will be no need to bother with an attenuator. In practice, however, there are often occasions when the quality of reception is spoiled by interference or some other 'breakthrough' transmission which manages to interrupt the original message at a critical point.

Some modern scanners are provided with a built-in attenuator, perhaps with a value of 10 or 20 decibels, which is brought into the circuit simply by pressing the appropriate button or by using a slide switch on the receiver.

The attenuator, when switched in to the circuit, immediately reduces the signal strength. If part of the transmission is weak, it will probably be eliminated entirely when the attenuator is used.

For more flexibility, and for those receivers that do not contain a built-in attenuator, it is possible to purchase individual attenuators for several values, which can be fitted either singly or in tandem to provide a variety of optional degrees of attenuation.

Attenuators are approximately 20mm in length, of tubular shape, roughly the same diameter as the coaxial cable. They are plugged directly into the aerial socket on the receiver, either singly or in multiples, to give the required level of reduction. The aerial coaxial lead is then connected to the attenuator, so that any signals are reduced in value before they reach the receiver.

The attenuators can be used in any combination — if a 3dB and two 6dB attenuators are purchased, it is possible to use them in varying selections to give attenuations of 3, 6, 9, 12 and 15 decibels — usually more than enough for most situations.

Attenuators are normally supplied with BNC connections as standard, being appropriate for use with the majority of VHF/UHF scanners.

If interference or unwanted 'breakthrough' signals are a problem, try fitting one or more attenuators to see if there is any improvement. It really is a question of experimentation until the right balance can be found.

Using a hand-held scanner with an external aerial can sometimes cause the circuitry within the set to become overloaded by certain signals and the use of an attenuator in these situations can be a positive advantage.

Amplifiers
Improved reception can often be achieved by using an attenuator. Alternatively (and surprisingly) it may be found that reception improvements can be made by amplifying the signal, rather than trying to reduce it. This feature of airband listening is covered next.

For those who are in areas of the country where reception on UHF or VHF is poor, perhaps because of the surrounding terrain or because the transmitters are too distant, it is

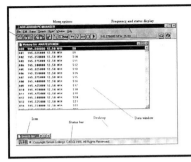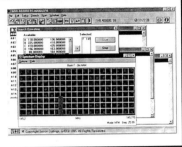

Above:
PC Manager for Windows is an-easy-to-use software package for the AOR AR8000 or AR2700 hand-portable radio receivers. *AOR*

Below:
The Hawk 5000 for Windows is a specialist software package designed to communicate with the AOR SDU5000 spectrum display unit and the AOR AR3000A, AR5000, and ICOM R7000, R7100, and R9000. *AOR*

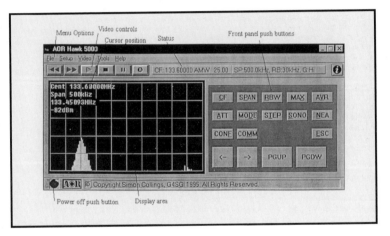

Below:
Electronic flight progress strips, as in this example, will replace paper strips at the new Swanwick Centre. This strip is for Britannia 662C flying at FL330 from Birmingham to Larnaca.
Civil Aviation Authority

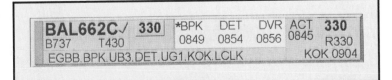

sometimes possible to improve the signal by the use of a separate amplifier which is introduced into the system between the antenna and the receiver (usually close to the receiver).

The amplifier has to be powered either from the mains or from a battery. Unfortunately, they cannot be relied upon to work in all situations. Experience has shown that, in some cases, they are actually detrimental and in fact produce results which are far worse than those experienced without amplification.

As with other ATC equipment it is a case of trial and error. It might be that one particular unit will work well in one area but not in another; however, it is not possible to predict where the 'good' and 'bad' areas might be. Trial and error is the only option, so your supplier should agree to a refund if the results are disappointing.

Amplifiers increase the intensity of the signal received via the antenna. Sometimes the effect is merely to increase interference to an unbearable level, where increasing the squelch to its maximum has no effect. In other cases, transmissions which might not otherwise be heard will be detected with quite reasonable results.

What is surprising is that normal reception, with various kinds of interference and 'breakthrough', can actually be improved by fitting an amplifier, and then reducing the squelch.

One further combination is possible — the use of an amplifier to boost the signal, while at the same time toning down its intensity by using an attenuator. Unfortunately, there are no hard and fast rules for using amplifiers or attenuators, except that it is unwise to assume that the most costly are the best!

Using Tape Recorders
Most airband listeners will be able to expand their knowledge and have more enjoyment if air traffic control messages are recorded. Not only will this enable the listener to analyse specific situations by reviewing a particular message or group of messages, it will also permit a record of activity to be made during periods when it is inconvenient for the listener to spend time listening 'live' to the receiver.

Undoubtedly the beginner will benefit more than most by being able to listen carefully, sentence by sentence, to every message and phrase in order to learn more about what is going on. Most newcomers to airband listening find the rapid clipped speech used by controllers and pilots very difficult to follow. Add to this the wide use of standard phrases and abbreviations, and the problem becomes even greater. Many experienced listeners probably do not realise how much of a message they are actually missing until the same sentences are played back later.

Another major advantage in using a tape recorder for airband messages is the ability to capture certain types of infrequent transmissions which the listener is very unlikely to hear during the normal periods of listening.

The use of a voice-activated tape recorder is the best method for detecting these occasional messages. The unit is set to record in the normal way, but if no sounds are detected the motor will be switched off about three seconds and the tape will remain stationary.

When a sound is detected — the voice of a controller or a pilot, for example — the motor is switched on and the tape starts to record. As long as the conversation continues the unit will record. At the end of a phrase or sentence the motor will continue to run for approximately three seconds. If no sound occurs during that period the motor will stop again.

The tape can be checked later for any messages and it will then be possible to listen to a tape which contains all the messages with virtually no break between them. If no messages have been detected during that period the tape will still be in its original position.

Some tape recorders are provided with a built-in voice-activated system which can be brought into operation at the flick of a switch. One or two airband receivers have voice-operated switching actually provided within the receiver so that they can be connected directly to an ordinary recorder.

Tape Recorder Connections
A further problem often experienced with airband receivers concerns the type of tape recorder connection. Few scanners have tape recorder outlets. Many are provided with outlets for extension speakers or earphones, but these are grossly overpowered for use with a tape recorder. It is therefore essential to reduce the power from an extension speaker outlet to a level which is appropriate to the tape recorder if undistorted results are required.

This is in fact quite simple and inexpensive, and is achieved by inserting a resistor into the centre core of the lead between the receiver and the recorder, with the result that the recordings will be clear and undistorted. Resistors are very inexpensive items and two or three of different values can be purchased for less than a pound. As a suggestion, try a resistor with a value of 100K as a start. If the results are not to your liking, try one of a higher or lower value. They take only minutes to fit and are well worth the expense in terms of improved quality. They can be bought from most radio shops (eg Tandy) and are simply soldered to the centre core of the recorder cable.

Another problem with using a receiver which is not provided with a tape recorder socket is the loss of reception when a tape lead is plugged in.

In other words, inserting the tape lead cuts out the signal to the receiver's loudspeaker, so that it is not possible to hear what is being recorded. (This does not happen with tape recorder outlets which do allow the listener to hear what is being said.)

This problem can be overcome quite easily by using a 'splitter' which is plugged into the outlet on the radio receiver. This actually splits the signal so that one connection can be made to the tape recorder while the other connection is made to a separate loudspeaker. It is therefore possible to produce a tape recording while listening to the actual messages via the separate external loudspeaker.

It is well worth playing about with tape recorders and voice-operated systems. Very good results can be obtained provided some thought is given to developing the end product and there is no doubt that many items of interest that would otherwise be missed can be captured and analysed.

Airborne Communication Addressing and Reporting System (ACARS)

Possession of an airband receiver enables the aviation enthusiast to become involved in a new and interesting aspect of the hobby. Most of the world's large airlines now use a digital message transmission system, known as ACARS, to send information back to base. Messages are sent by VHF datalink, in short bursts of digitally processed information usually lasting no more than half a second. The European frequency is 131.725MHz.

Decoding equipment on the ground converts the signal back to its original format in a series of coded letters and numbers. Sometimes the message is sent by the crew, others are automatically prompted by predetermined events on the aircraft — for example, raising the undercarriage sends a departure message, releasing the brakes prompts an off-blocks message, and so on. Included every time, of course, are the aircraft details — airline flight number and registration — and this information is particularly useful to the aircraft spotter.

Anyone can purchase the equipment to decode the messages. The VHF receiver is connected to the unit and the datalink messages can then be printed or alternatively viewed on a standard personal computer. Unfortunately, the messages can be extremely lengthy and they are further complicated by the fact that various airlines use different message formats.

Another system suitable for the data reception of aeronautical ACARS information is available through a completely stand-alone piece of equipment from AOR, the ARD-2 decoder and display unit. This provides portable operation from internal batteries or from an external twelve volt power supply without the need for a computer. The built-in LCD provides two lines of text with up to 32 characters of text per line and a scroll back buffer of 512 characters. A suitable scanner is connected to the unit with a single cable and the receiver set to the European frequency of 131.725MHz.

The unit then displays any ACARS messages on the display, thereby offering the enthusiast a whole new range of interesting information about flights in the area.

The receiving equipment on the ground has sophisticated facilities for detecting errors in a message and, of course, it is possible that more than one transmission will be made at the same time. This means that the data can be sent several times in quick succession before being accepted, resulting in pages of useless information for the airband listener.

Below:
The Data Master is a windows-based PC package which provides IBM control of the AOR AR7030 and AR3030. *AOR*

Above:
Sea Harrier FRS 2. *British Aerospace*

At least one programme is now available which analyses each message and selects only the vital information — airline, callsign, registration and time. This can be stored and used as and when required or printed out as a report for each particular period of time. By this method the aircraft spotter has a ready-made listing for all flights heard and reports can be produced in numerous forms.

For full details of the system contact the suppliers in Appendix X.

Selective Calling (SELCAL) Analysis
Another area of possible interest is the ability to determine the identity of a flight by decoding its SELCAL. This is a four digit number unique to each aircraft and is used by HF radio operators to make contact with the crew.

SELCALs consist of two pairs of letters which are transmitted to the aircraft. It is possible to purchase a decoder which receives the signal on HF and indicates on a panel readout the actual letters, enabling the enthusiast to identify the aircraft from a printed table.

Computer Control
A few scanners now have the facility for being managed through a personal computer. The receiver is connected to the PC via a special connecting lead and an interface unit. Frequencies can be entered and sorted on the computer and downloaded to the receiver's

memory. Various kinds of reports can also be produced.

It is doubtful if this arrangement is appropriate for the listener whose only interest is in airband, since the need to manage and rearrange frequencies is relatively rare. Also, of course, access to a PC is required and the interface and software are not particularly cheap.

For further details contact one of the suppliers in Appendix X.

Frequency Counters
Electronic devices are available to the airband listener for automatically scanning the radio spectrum to locate any nearby transmissions, with the actual frequency being displayed and stored on an LCD readout.

These devices sweep between 30MHz through to 2GHz in less than one second, automatically locking onto any frequency (not just airband) which can then be downloaded to a scanner or to a computer with the appropriate interface. For the airband listener, they are only really suitable for airport use as the range is limited to relatively short distances.

Appendix I: VHF and UHF Airband Receivers

Most receivers which are available today for aeronautical use are covered in this appendix. In many cases the range of frequencies is far wider than those required purely for aviation, covering, for example, marine and the broadcast bands. If your interest is related only to air traffic messages go for a dedicated scanner as invariably this will give better results.

There is a growing tendency to produce receivers which are more and more sophisticated, covering a very wide range of frequencies as opposed to dedicated airband models. Remember also that high cost does not necessarily mean better results.

Before deciding on a particular purchase consider the following points:

■ check the details with the supplier, since receivers with the same name and model number may have different specifications depending on when and where they were produced;
■ speak to one or more of the suppliers whose details are included in the appendices;
■ look out for special offers but check carefully that the features you require are covered;
■ try and persuade your supplier to let you have a receiver on trial — some do have a policy for accepting returns or exchanges.

The prices quoted are an approximate guide for 1999. However, variations do occur, particularly when models are at the end of their production or when special prices are on offer.

ALINCO DJ-X10
Hand-held wide-band receiver covering civil, military and HF airbands; 1,200 memories in 30 banks. Frequency steps ranging from 50Hz to 500kHz. A wide-band scanner which can be tuned to the 8.33 channels.
Price guide: £300

AOR AR-1500
Hand-held wide-band receiver covering civil, military and HF airbands; 1,000 memories in 10 banks (including automatic storage of all active channels if required). Frequency steps — programmable in steps of 5 or 12.5kHz up to 995kHz. Unable to receive the proposed 8.33kHz channels. Includes a built-in attenuator.
Price guide: £195

AOR AR-2700
Hand-held wide-band scanner covering civil and military airbands; 500 memories in 10 banks. Frequency steps (in kilohertz): 5, 6.25, 9, 10,

12.5, 25, 50, 100. A popular model produced by one of the most reputable companies in the business. The receiver has an optional facility for recording transmissions built into the set (around 5 seconds duration).
Price guide: £175

AOR AR-3000A
A professional standard base station covering all aeronautical channels; 400 memories in four banks. Frequency steps from 1kHz upwards. A high-quality base receiver with the ability to tune to the 8.33 range of channels.
Price guide: £700

AOR AR-5000
Mains-operated base station with the ability to receive the full airband range — civilian VHF, military UHF and HF shortwave, 1,000 memories in 20 banks. Frequency steps (in kilohertz), all modes have steps in multiples of 1 hertz. This is a high performance receiver capable of receiving all aeronautical transmissions, including the proposed 8.33kHz range. The set is fitted with a tape recorder facility and a built-in attenuator and also computer control if required. However, the cost is high for the airband listener.
Price guide: £1,750

AOR AR-8000
A sophisticated high-specification hand-held wide-band scanner covering civilian VHF, military UHF and HF shortwave; 1,000 memories in 20 banks. Frequency steps (in kilohertz): 0.1 up to 995kHz in increments of 50 hertz. Another top of the range receiver capable of receiving the proposed 8.33kHz transmissions and also airport repeaters. Provided with a programmable attenuator and the addition of text to indicate individual channels. Suitable for computer control if required. The only drawback is that it is probably too complex for the beginner.
Price guide: £350

AOR AR-8200
A new and even more sophisticated high specification hand-held wide-band scanner covering all frequencies; 1,000 memories in 20 banks capable of being increased to 4,000 memories. Frequency steps from 0.1kHz upwards. A very sophisticated wide-band scanner with 8.33 channel spacing built in. Computer control is available, together with many other sophisticated features.
Price guide: £375

COMMTEL 202

Hand-held civil airband scanner. Fifty memories (no banks). Frequency steps (in kilohertz) pre-set at 5, 12.5 and 25. A good value model for the beginner.

Price guide: £95

COMMTEL 213

A dedicated civil airband hand-held receiver; 100 memories in 10 banks.

Price guide: £150

COMMTEL 214

Hand-held civil airband scanner. n/a. memories (no banks). Another popular model for dedicated use.

Price guide: £135

COMMTEL 510

A miniature VHF and UHF civil and military airband hand-held receiver; 800 memories in 20 banks. Frequency steps from 1kHz through to 100kHz.

Price guide: £190

ICOM IC-R2

A miniature VHF and UHF civil and military airband hand-held receiver; 400 memories in 8 banks. Frequency steps from 5 to 100kHz.

Price guide: £115

ICOM IC-R10

Hand-held wide-band receiver covering civil, military and HF airbands; 1,000 memories in 10 banks. Frequency steps from ·1 to 100kHz. A new model with the latest features including a built-in 20dB attenuator, and facilities for computer control.

Price guide: £400

JETSTREAM

A basic hand-held receiver with no sophistication. Only suitable for airport or very localised use.

Price guide: £20

PSR 244

A dedicated civil airband hand-held receiver; 50 memories.

Price guide: £125

REALISTIC PRO-60

A hand-held scanner suitable for civilian and military airband and airport repeaters; 200 memories in 10 banks. Frequency steps (in kilohertz) pre-set at 5, 12.5 and 25. Receives in AM, narrow FM and wide FM modes. Unable to accept 8.33kHz channels.

Price range: £200

REALISTIC PRO-62

Hand-held scanner covering civil airband only; 200 memories in 10 banks. Unable to receive proposed 8.33kHz channels.

Price guide: £200

REALISTIC PRO-63

Hand-held scanner covering civil airband only; 100 memories in 10 banks. Unable to receive proposed 8.33kHz channels.

Price guide: £150

REALISTIC PRO-26

Hand-held scanner covering civilian and military airband and airport repeaters; 200 memories in 10 banks. Frequency steps (in kilohertz) pre-set at 5, 12.5 and 25.

Price range: £300

REALISTIC PRO-25

Hand-held scanner covering civilian and military airband; 100 memories in 10 banks. Frequency steps (in kilohertz) 5, 25 (factory set).

Price range: £175

REALISTIC PRO-2039

Base station scanner covering civilian and military airband; 200 memories in 10 banks. Frequency steps (in kilohertz) pre-set at 5, 12.5 and 25.

Price range: £200

REALISTIC PRO-2042

Hand-held wide-band receiver covering civil and military airbands. HF n/k; 1,000 memories in 10 banks.

Price guide: £345

SCANAP

A dedicated hand-held airband receiver for civil and military bands; 100 memories. Frequency steps 12.5kHz and 8.33kHz. One of the few scanners available specifically designed with the 8.33 bands in mind.

Price guide: n/a

SONY AIR 7 (MK II)

Hand-held scanner for civilian airband; 10 memories per band. Frequency steps (in kilohertz) pre-set to suit band selected. This model covers four wave bands including airband VHF with 25kHz steps, limited to only 10 memories.

Price range: £295

SONY ICF PRO 80

Hand-held HF scanner. Note that civil airband requires the use of a separate conversion unit FRQ-80; 40 memories in four banks. Frequency steps (in kilohertz) 1 (factory set).

Price guide: £345

SKYVOICE

A basic model hand-held civil airband receiver. A simple-to-use beginners' model but lacking any sophisticated features.

Price guide: £95

STEEPLETONE SAB 9/SAB 11/SAB 12

Steepletone produces three airband radio receivers eminently suitable for newcomers to the hobby. Each model covers medium wave and FM radio. Two models cover marine radio as well. The SAB 12 model is provided with a squelch facility. Because these receivers are of the continuous tuning type, they can handle the proposed 8.33kHz channels.

Price guide: SAB 11 £18, SAB 9 £27, SAB 12 £33

TRIDENT TR-2400

Hand-held model with wide frequency range covering civilian and military airbands, HF (shortwave) upper side band and airport repeaters;. 1,000 memories in 10 banks. Frequency steps (in kilohertz): multiples of 1kHz. An all-mode reception receiver with rotary or keypad frequency control and fast scan. Capable of receiving 8.33kHz channels.

Price range: £300

TRIDENT TR-1200

Hand-held scanner with wide frequency range (not continuous) covering civilian and military airbands and airport repeaters; 1,000 memories in 10 banks. Frequency steps (in kilohertz): from 5kHz upwards in multiples of 5 or 12.5 up to 995. This model receives in AM, narrow FM and wide FM modes with rotary or keypad frequency control. However, not capable of receiving the proposed 8.33 kilohertz channels.

Price range: £300

TRIDENT TR - 980

A hand-held scanner capable of receiving civilian and military airbands and airport repeaters; 125 memories in five banks. Frequency steps (in kilohertz) 5, 10, 12.5, 25 and 30. This model receives in AM, narrow FM, wide FM modes with rotary or keypad frequency control. However, not capable of receiving the proposed 8.33kHz channels.

Price range: £195

UNIDEN BEARCAT BC860XLT

Base station wide-band scanner covering the civilian VHF airband; 100 memories in 10 banks. Frequency steps (in kilohertz): 5, 12.5 (factory set). A reasonably priced receiver with high-speed scan and search but unable to receive 8.33kHz channels.

Price guide: £145

UNIDEN BEARCAT BC9000XLT

Base station wide-band scanner capable of receiving civilian VHF and military UHF airbands; 500 memories in 20 banks. Frequency steps (in kilohertz): 5, 12.5, 25, 50. Receives in AM, narrow FM and wide FM modes. Selectable attenuator, automatic tape recording feature and high speed scan and search are among its features, but is unable to receive 8.33kHz channels.

Price guide: £325

UNIDEN BEARCAT BC120XLT

Hand-held scanner capable of receiving civilian VHF airband; 100 memories in 10 banks. Frequency steps (in kilohertz): 5, 12.5 (factory set). Features high-speed scan and search with 10 priority channels, but is unable to receive 8.33kHz channels. Requires a special rechargeable battery pack.

Price guide: £140

UNIDEN BEARCAT UBC220XLT

Hand-held scanner capable of receiving civilian VHF airband; 200 memories in 10 banks. Frequency steps (in kilohertz): 5, 12.5 (factory set). A reasonably priced scanner operating on batteries only, but unable to receive 8.33kHz channels. Requires a special rechargeable battery pack.

Price guide: £195

UNIDEN BEARCAT UBC3000XLT

Hand-held scanner capable of receiving civilian VHF and military UHF airband and airport repeaters; 400 memories in 10 banks. Frequency steps (in kilohertz): 5, 12.5, 50. Receives in AM, narrow FM and wide FM modes, and features high-speed search and scan, but unable to receive 8.33kHz channels.

Price guide: £250

WELZ WS-2000

A miniature hand-held sophisticated scanner with many of the latest features, including the ability to receive the proposed 8.33kHz channels; 800 memories in 10 banks. Frequency steps (in kilohertz): 1, 5, 6.25, 9, 10, 12.5, 15, 20, 25, 30, 50 and 100. Perhaps too complex for the beginner.

Price guide: £275

WIN 108

Hand-held dedicated scanner for civilian VHF airband now only available on the secondhand market; 20 memories in two banks. Frequency steps (in kilohertz): 25. A basic inexpensive scanner although early models did not extend beyond 136.0 megahertz. Unable to receive 8.33kHz channels.

Price guide: £100 (depending on condition)

YUPITERU VT125

A dedicated hand-held scanner from one of the best known companies in the airband business. Suitable for civilian VHF airband; 30 memories in 1 bank. Frequency steps (in kilohertz): 25, 50, 100. A very popular and efficient receiver, although unable to receive the 8.33kHz channels.

Price guide: £125 (secondhand)

YUPITERU VT225

A dedicated hand-held scanner covering civilian VHF and military UHF airbands and also marine frequencies; 100 memories in 10 banks. Frequency steps (in kilohertz): 10, 12.5, 25, 50, 100. Another popular choice and easy to use. Unable to receive the 8.33kHz channels.

Price guide: £200 (secondhand)

YUPITERU MVT3300

A dedicated civil airband hand-held scanner from one of the best known manufacturers; 200 memories in 10 banks. Frequency steps in kHz: 5, 6.25, 10, 12.5, 25. Although this model was introduced in 1998, it does not have the facility for the 8.33kHz channels.

Price guide: £150

YUPITERU MVT6000

Mains-operated base station wide-band scanner covering civilian VHF airband and military UHF airband and airport repeaters; 100 memories in 5 banks. Frequency steps (in kilohertz): 5, 10, 12.5, 25. Unable to receive 8.33kHz channels.

Price guide: £150 (secondhand)

YUPITERU MVT7000

Hand-held wide range scanner capable of receiving civilian VHF and military UHF airbands and also airport repeaters; 200 memories in 10 banks. Frequency steps (in kilohertz): 5, 10, 12.5, 25, 50, 100. Another popular choice with the feature of rotary tuning, but unable to receive 8.33kHz channels.

Price guide: £200 (secondhand)

YUPITERU MVT7100

Hand-held wide range scanner capable of receiving civilian VHF, military UHF and HF shortwave aeronautical bands. Note that this model is also known as the MVT 7100EX. 1,000 memories in 10 banks. Frequency steps (in kilohertz): 1, 5, 6.25, 10, 12.5, 20, 25, 50, 100 (for HF steps are 50 or 100 hertz). This receiver operates across the entire aeronautical range, including airport repeaters and the proposed 8.33kHz channels. However shortwave reception cannot be expected to match the performance of dedicated HF receivers.

Price guide: £300

YUPITERU MVT7200 EX

An improved version of the MVT7100 model. Covers civil, military and HF airbands. 1,000 memories in 10 banks. Frequency steps as for the 7100.

Price guide: £300

YUPITERU MVT8000

Base or mobile scanning receiver covering civil and military airbands including airport repeaters, but not the proposed 8.33kHz channels; 200 memories in 10 banks. Frequency steps (in kilohertz): 5, 10, 12.5, 25, 50, 100.

Price guide: £400

YUPITERU MVT9000

Hand-held wide-band receiver covering civil, military and HF airbands; 1,000 memories in 20 banks, with alpha numeric 'labelling' of stations. Frequency steps 50, 100, 200Hz, 1, 5, 6.25, 8, 9, 10, 12.5, 15, 20, 25, 30, 50, 100, 125kHz. A top of the range receiver with all the latest facilities, including tuning to 8.33kHz channels.

Note Regarding 8.33kHz Channels

References to a receiver's ability to tune to the proposed new channel spacings are based on the provision of steps of 1kHz or less. In such cases it will be possible to select a frequency with an accuracy of at least 1kHz and then to store the channel in the memory. For example, the AR-8000 can be tuned to 127.0083 and this can then be stored. However, it will not be possible to search for the new channels unless the receiver is provided with steps equal to the new channel spacings.

HF (Shortwave) Receivers

Readers who may be contemplating the purchase of a receiver for HF listening are advised to discuss the matter with one of the suppliers listed in Appendix X, since the subject is rather specialised and can be somewhat complex.

Below:
AOR AR7030 communications receiver. AOR

Appendix II: Airfield Directory

Airfield	Service	VHF	UHF
Aberdeen/Dyce	App	120. 4	353.55
	Radar	128. 3	
		121.25	
	Tower	118. 1	
	Gnd	121. 7	
	ATIS (VOR 'ADN)	121.85	
Aberporth	AFIS	122.15	259. 0
Alderney	App (Guernsey)	128.65	
	Tower	125.35	
Baldonnel/Casement	App	122. 0	
	Radar	122. 8	
	Talkdown	129. 7	
	Dublin Military	122. 3	
	Tower	123. 5	
	Gnd	123. 1	
Barkston Heath	App (Cranwell)		340.47
	Director		261.05
	Departures		291. 7
	Talkdown		360.72
	Tower	120.42	342.07
	Gnd		340.52
	ATIS		269. 9
Belfast/Aldergrove	App	120. 9	310.00
		120. 0	
	Radar	120. 9	310.00
	Tower	118. 3	310.00
	Gnd	121.75	
	Ops (RAF)		241.82
	ATIS	128. 2	
Belfast City	App	130.85	
	Tower	130.75	
	ATIS	136.62	
Benbecula	App/Tower	119. 2	
Benson	CAC (Brize)	134. 3	257. 1
	App	127.15	268.82
	SRE (Benson Zone)	120. 9	362. 3
	SRE (Benson Director)	122. 1	315.75
	Talkdown	123. 3	259.87
	Tower	130.25	279.35
	Gnd		340.32
	ATIS		241.62
Biggin Hill	App	129. 4	
	Tower	134. 8	
	ATIS	121.87	

Airfield	Service	VHF	UHF
Birmingham	App	118.05	
	Tower	118.3	
	Gnd	121.8	
	ATIS	126.27	
Blackbushe	AFIS	122.3	
Blackpool	Tower	118.4	
	App	119.95	
	Radar	135.95	
	ATIS	121.75	
Boscombe Down	App/SRE	126.7	359.77
	Departures		276.85
	Director	130.0	291.65
	Zone		362.65
	Talkdown		336.15
	Tower	130.75	370.1
	Gnd	130.75	299.4
	ATIS		263.5
Bournemouth	App	119.62	
	Tower	125.6	
	Radar	118.65	
	Gnd	121.7	
	ATIS	121.95	
Bristol	App	128.55	
	Radar	124.35	
	Tower	133.85	
	ATIS	126.02	
Brize Norton	MAS/LARS/CAC	134.3	257.1
(Brize Radar)	App	127.25	342.45
			362.3
	SRE (Director)	124.27	356.87
	SRE (Talkdown)	123.72	338.65
			385.4
	Tower	126.5	396.7
			257.8
	Zone	119.0	
	Gnd	121.72	370.3
	Ops	130.07	357.47
	ATIS		254.47
Cambridge	App	123.6	
	Radar	130.75	372.42
	Tower	122.2	372.42
Cardiff	App	125.85	277.22
	Radar	124.1	
	Tower	125.0	
	ATIS	119.47	
Carlisle	App/Tower	123.6	

Airfield	Service	VHF	UHF
Church Fenton	App	126. 5	254.52
	SRE		362. 3
	SRE (Director)		344. 0
			375.32
	PAR (Talkdown)	123. 3	386.72
			385. 4
	Tower	122. 1	257. 8
	Gnd	122. 1	340. 2
Colerne	App	122. 1	277.27
			362. 3
	Tower	122. 1	258.97
	Gnd		360.75
Coltishall	CAC (Eastern)		299.97
	App	122. 1	315.32
	SRE (Director)	123. 3	342.25
	SRE (Zone)	125. 9	293.42
	PAR (Talkdown)	123. 3	275.97
	Tower	122. 1	339.95
	Gnd		387.77
	Ops		364. 8
Coningsby	CAC		299.97
	App	120. 8	312.22
			362. 3
			344.62
	SRE		262.95
			344. 0
	PAR (Talkdown)	123. 3	300.92
			337.97
	Tower	122. 1	275.87
		119.97	
	Gnd	122. 1	358.55
Cork	App	119. 9	
	Radar	118. 8	
	Tower	119. 3	
		121. 7	
	Gnd	121. 8	
	ATIS	120.92	
Cosford	App	118.92	276.12
	Tower	118.92	357.12
	Gnd	121.95	
Cottesmore	CAC		299.97
	App	130. 2	312.07
			340.57
	App (Wittering)	123. 3	388.52
	SRE (Director)	123. 3	312.07
			358.72
			376.57
	PAR (Talkdown)	123. 3	262. 9
			337.87
	Tower	122. 1	370.05
			257. 8
	Gnd	122. 1	336.37
	ATIS		243.32

Airfield	Service	VHF	UHF
Coventry	App	119.25	
	Radar	122. 0	
	Tower	119.25	
		124.8	
	Gnd	121. 7	
Cranfield	App	122.85	
	Tower	134.92	
	ATIS	121.87	
Cranwell	MAS		299.97
	App	119.37	340.47
			362. 3
	SRE (Radar)		250.05
	SRE (Director)	123. 3	282. 0
			344. 0
	PAR (Talkdown)	123. 3	356.92
	Tower	122. 1	379.52
			257. 8
	Gnd		297. 9
	ATIS	135.67	247.17
Culdrose	App	134.05	241.95
	Radar	122. 1	241.95
	PAR (Talkdown)	123. 3	388. 0
	Tower	122. 1	386.52
	Gnd		299. 4
	ATIS		282. 1

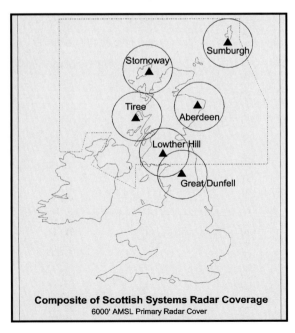

Composite of Scottish Systems Radar Coverage
6000' AMSL Primary Radar Cover

Left:
Locations of radar
stations in Scotland.
*Civil Aviation
Authority*

Airfield	Service	VHF	UHF
Dishforth	App	125. 0	357.37
			362. 3
	Tower	122. 1	259.82
	Gnd	122. 1	379.67
Dublin	App	121. 1	
		118. 5	
	Radar	124.65	
		129.17	
		136.05	
		136.15	
	SRE	119.55	
	Tower	118. 6	
	Delivery Clearance	121.87	
	Gnd	121. 8	
	ATIS	124.52	
Dundee	App	122. 9	
	Tower	122. 9	
Dunsfold	CAC (London)		275.47
	App	135.17	367.37
			312.62
	SRE	135.17	367.37
		122.55	
	Tower	124.32	375. 4
East Midlands	App	119.65	
		120.12	
	Tower	124. 0	
	Gnd	121. 9	
	ATIS	128.22	
Edinburgh	App	121. 2	
	Radar	121. 2	
	Tower	118. 7	
	Gnd	121.75	
	ATIS	132.07	
Exeter	App	128.15	
		119.05	
	Tower	119. 8	
Fairford	CAC (Brize)	134. 3	257. 1
	App	122. 1	342.45
			362. 3
	SRE (Brize)	119. 0	376.62
	Tower	119.15	337.57
	Gnd		259.97
	Ops		379.47
	Metro		257.75
Farnborough	App	134.35	376. 9
	Radar	125.25	315.52
	PAR	130.05	259. 0
	Tower	122. 5	357. 4
	Ops	130.37	

Airfield	Service	VHF	UHF
Filton	App	122.72	256.12
		127.97	
	SRE	122.72	256.12
	Tower	132.35	342.02
Glasgow	App	119. 1	362. 3
	Radar	119. 3	
	Tower	118. 8	
	Gnd	121. 7	
	ATIS	129.57	
Gloucestershire	App	125.65	
	Tower	122. 9	
	Radar	120.97	
	ATIS	127.47	
Guernsey	App	128.65	
		124. 5	
	Radar	118. 9	
	Tower	119.95	
	Gnd	121. 8	
	ATIS (GUR) VOR	109. 4	
Hawarden	App	123.35	
	Radar	130.25	
	Tower	124.95	336.32
Honington	Lakenheath Radar	128. 9	264.67
	Lakenheath App	128. 9	337. 6
	App	123. 3	254.87
			309.95
			257. 8
			315.57
	SRE/PAR		309.95
			358.75
	NATO/Director		344. 0
	NATO/Talkdown	123. 3	385. 4
	Tower	122. 1	282.27
	Gnd/Ops		241.97
Humberside	Radar	123.15	
	App	124.67	
	Tower	118.55	
	ATIS	124.12	
Inverness	App	122. 6	362. 3
	Tower	122. 6	
Isle of Man	App	120.85	
(Ronaldsway)	Radar	118. 2	
		125. 3	
	Tower	118. 9	
Jersey	Zone	125. 2	
		120.45	
	Radar	118.55	
	App	120. 3	
	Tower	119.45	
	Gnd	121. 9	
	ATIS (JSY) VOR	112. 2	
	Jersey Information	129.72	

Airfield	Service	VHF	UHF
Kinloss	App (Lossiemouth)	119.35	376.65
	SRE	123. 3	259.97
			311.32
	PAR (Talkdown)	123. 3	370.05
			376.52
	Tower	122. 1	336.35
			257. 8
	Ops		358.47
	Gnd		296.72
Kirkwall	App	118. 3	
	Tower	118. 3	
Lakenheath	CAC		299.97
	App (Honington)	128. 9	
	App (Departures)	123. 3	242.07
	SRE	123. 3	309.07
	Tower	122. 1	358.67
			257. 8
	Gnd		397.97
	Ops		300.82
	ATIS		249. 7

Below:
Manchester ATCC. *Civil Aviation Authority*

Airfield	Service	VHF	UHF
Leeds/Bradford	App	123.75	
	SRE	121.05	
	Tower	120. 3	
	ATIS	118.02	
Leeming	App	127.75	337.82
	SRE (Zone)	127.75	292. 7
	SRE (Director)	127.75	358.65
			344. 0
	PAR (Talkdown)	123. 3	336.35
			309.87
			385. 4
	Tower	122. 1	344.57
			257. 8
	Gnd		386.52
	Ops		356.72
Leicester	Air/Gnd	122.12	
Leuchars	App	126. 5	255. 4
			362. 3
	SRE (Director)	123. 3	292.47
	PAR (Talkdown)	123. 3	370.07
	Tower	122. 1	259.12
	Gnd	122. 1	297. 9
	Ops		285.02
Linton-on-Ouse	App	129.15	362.67
	SRE (Radar)	129.15	292. 8
	SRE (Director)	123. 3	344.47
	SRE (Departures)	129.15	277.62
	PAR (Talkdown)	123. 3	358.52
	Tower	122. 1	257. 8
	Gnd	122. 1	340.02
	ATIS		241.65
Liverpool	App	119.85	
	Radar	118.45	
	Tower	118. 1	
Llanbedr	CAC (London)		292.52
	App	122. 5	386.67
	PAR	122. 5	370. 3
	Tower	122. 5	387.75
London/City	App (Thames Radar)	132. 7	
	Radar	128.02	
	Tower	127.95	
		118.07	
	ATIS	127.95	
London/Gatwick	App	126.82	
		118.95	
		135.57	
		129.02	
	Tower	124.22	
		134.22	
	Clearances	121.95	
	Gnd	121. 8	
	ATIS	136.52	

Airfield	Service	VHF	UHF
London/Heathrow	App	119.72	
		134.97	
		120. 4	
		127.52	
	Radar	119. 9	
		125.62	
	Tower (Departures)	118. 7	
	Tower (Arrivals)	118. 5	
	Clearances	121.97	
	Gnd	121. 9	
	ATIS	123. 9	
	ATIS — Biggin VOR	115. 1	
	ATIS — Bovingdon VOR	113.75	
London/Luton	App	129.55	
		126.72	
	Radar	128.75	
	Tower	132.55	
	Gnd	121.75	
	ATIS	120.57	
London/Stansted	App (Essex Radar)	120.62	
		126.95	
	Tower	123. 8	
		125.55	
	Gnd	121.72	
	ATIS	114.55	
Lossiemouth	App	376.65	
		362. 3	
	SRE	123. 3	259.97
			311.32
	SRE (Departures)	119.35	258.85
	PAR (Talkdown)	123. 3	250.05
			312. 4
	Tower	118. 9	337.75
		122. 1	
	Gnd		299. 4
	ATIS		269.02
Lyneham	CAC (London)		275.47
	CAC (Brize)	134. 3	257. 1
	App	118.42	359. 5
			362. 3
	SRE (Zone)	123. 4	345.02
	SRE (Director)	123. 4	300.47
			344. 0
	PAR (Talkdown)	123. 3	375. 2
			385. 4
	Tower	118.42	386.82
	Gnd	122. 1	340.17
	Ops		254.65
	ATIS		277.92

Airfield	Service	VHF	UHF
Manchester	Area Control	124. 2	
	Area Control	125. 1	
	Area Control	123. 4	
		126.65	
		125.95	
	Pennine Radar	128.67	
	App	119. 4	
	Director	121.35	
	Arrivals	118.57	
	Tower	118.62	
	Clearances	121. 7	
	Gnd	121. 7	
	ATIS	128.17	
Manston	CAC (London)		275.47
	App	126.35	379.02
			231. 6
			362. 3
	Radar	126.35	338.62
			344. 0
	PAR (Talkdown)	123. 3	312.32
	Tower	119.27	344.35
			257. 8
Marham	CAC		299.97
	App	124.15	268.87
			362. 3
	SRE (Radar)	124.15	293.77
			344. 0
	PAR (Talkdown)	123. 3	379.65
			385. 4
	Tower	122. 1	337. 9
			257. 8
	Gnd		336.35
	Ops		312.55
	ATIS		261. 2
Merryfield	Tower	122. 1	312. 7
Middle Wallop	App	118.27	312. 0
	SRE (Director)		312.67
	Talkdown		364.82
	Tower	118.27	372.62
Mildenhall	CAC		299.97
	App (Lakenheath)		337. 6
	Departures (Lakenheath)	137. 2	242.07
	Tower	122.55	370.25
	Gnd		278.15
	Ops		365. 1
			312.45
	ATIS		257.75
Netheravon	AFIS	128. 3	290.95
	A/G (Salisbury Plain)	122.75	282.25
Newcastle	App	124.37	284. 6
	Radar	118. 5	
	Tower	119. 7	
	ATIS	114.25	

Airfield	Service	VHF	UHF
Newton	App	122. 1	251.72
	Departures (Waddington)	127.35	296.75
	Tower	119.12	375.42
	Gnd		258.97
Northolt	App	126.45	344.97
			362. 3
	SRE (Director)	130.35	379.42
			375. 5
	PAR (Talkdown)	125.87	385. 4
	Tower	124.97	312.35
			257. 8
	Departures	120.32	
	Ops		244.42
	ATIS		300.35
Norwich	App	119.35	
	Radar	128.32	
	Tower	124.25	
	ATIS	128.62	
Nottingham	Air/Gnd	122. 8	
Odiham	App	125.25	386.77
	PAR (Talkdown)	123. 3	300.45
			385. 4
	Tower	122. 1	309.62
			257. 8
	ATIS		276.17
	FIS		315.97
Oxford/Kidlington	CAC (Brize)	134. 3	
	App	125.32	
	Tower	118.87	
	Gnd	121.95	
	ATIS	121.75	
	Information	118.87	

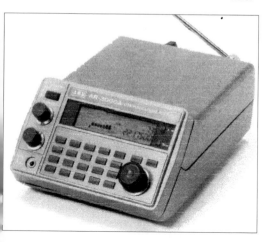

Left:
AOR AR3000 air band
receiver. *AOR*

Airfield	Service	VHF	UHF
Plymouth	App	133.55	
	Tower	122. 6	
Portland	App	124.15	300.17
			362. 3
	PAR (Talkdown)		312. 4
	Tower	122. 1	337.75
	ATIS		343.47
Prestwick	App	120.55	
	Radar	119.45	
	Tower	118.15	
		121. 8	
	ATIS	127.12	
St Athan	App (Cardiff)	125.85	277.22
	App (St Athan)	122. 1	357.17
			362. 3
	SRE (Talkdown)	123. 3	340. 1
			372.37
	Tower	122. 1	336.52
			257. 8
	Gnd		386. 5
	ATIS (Cardiff)	119.47	
St Mawgan	CAC (London)		275.47
	App	126. 5	357. 2
		122. 1	
	SRE (Director)	125.55	360.55
			344. 0
	PAR (Talkdown)	123. 3	387.45
			385. 4
	Gnd		376.62
	Tower	123. 4	241.82
	Ops		260. 0
	ATIS		252.52
Isles of Scilly/St Marys	App	123.15	
	Tower	123.15	
Shannon (Limerick)	App	120. 2	
	Radar	121. 4	
	Tower	118. 7	
	Clearances	121. 7	
	Gnd	121. 8	
	ATIS	130.95	
Shawbury	App	120.77	356.32
			362.47
	SRE (Zone)	120.77	
	SRE (Radar)	123. 3	254. 2
	PAR (Talkdown)	123. 3	356.97
			376.67
	Tower	122. 1	340.35
	Gnd		337. 9
	ATIS		292.57
Sheffield	App/Tower	128.52	
	ATIS	121. 7	

Airfield	Service	VHF	UHF
Shoreham	App	123.15	
	Tower	125. 4	
	ATIS	132. 4	
Southampton	App	128.85	
	Zone (Solent)	120.22	
	Radar	128.25	
	Tower	118. 2	
	ATIS (SAM) VOR	113.35	
	Ops	130.65	
Southend	App	128.95	
	Radar	125.05	
	Tower	127.72	
	ATIS	121. 8	
Stornoway	App	123. 5	
	Tower	123. 5	
Sumburgh	App/Radar	123.15	
	Tower	118.25	
	ATIS	125.85	
Swansea	App	119. 7	
	Tower	119. 7	
Teesside	App	118.85	296.72
	Radar	128.85	
	Tower	119. 8	379. 8
Ternhill	App (Shawbury)		356.32
	Talkdown	122. 1	311. 1
			372.57
	Tower	122. 1	338.82
Topcliffe	App	125. 0	357.37
			362. 3
	SRE (Talkdown)	123. 3	344.35
			385. 4
	SRE (Director)	125. 0	255. 6
			344. 0
	Tower	122. 1	309.72
			257. 8
	Gnd		387.45
Unst	Air/Gnd	130.35	
	Ops	123.45	
Valley	App	134.35	372.32
			362. 3
	SRE (Radar)	134.35	258.82
	SRE (Director)	123. 3	337.72
			344. 0
	PAR (Talkdown)	123. 3	358.67
			385. 4
	Tower	122. 1	340.17
			257. 8
	Gnd	122. 1	356.75

Airfield	Service	VHF	UHF
Waddington	CAC		299.97
	App		312. 5
			362. 3
	SRE (Radar)	127.35	296.75
		125.35	
	SRE (Director)	123. 3	300.57
	PAR (Talkdown)		309.67
			385. 4
	Departures	123. 3	249.85
	Tower	123. 3	388.22
			257. 8
	Gnd		342.12
	Ops		244.27
	ATIS		291.67
Warton	App	124.45	336.47
	SRE (Radar)	129.72	343. 7
	Tower	130. 8	311. 3
Waterford	Tower	129.85	
Wattisham	App	125. 8	291.12
	Dir	123. 3	283.57
	PAR	123. 3	356.17
			359.82
	Tower	122. 1	358. 6
West Freugh	App	130.05	260.02
	SRE (Radar)	130.72	259. 0
	Tower	122.55	337.92
Wick	App	119. 7	
	Tower	119. 7	
Wittering	CAC (Easterly)		299.97
	CAC (Westerly)		275.47
	App	130. 2	388.52
			362. 3
	SRE (Departures)		376.57
			344. 0
	PAR (Talkdown)	123. 3	396.85
			337.95
	Tower	118.15	357.15
	Gnd		311.95
Woodford	MAS		299.97
	App	130.75	269.12
	SRE	130.05	358.57
	Tower	126.92	358.57
Woodvale	App	121. 0	312. 8
	Tower	119.75	259.95
Yeovil (Judwin)	App	130. 8	369.97
	Radar	130. 8	300.67
	Tower	125. 4	372.42

Airfield	Service	VHF	UHF
Yeovilton	App	127.35	369.87
			362. 3
	Radar	127.35	369.87
	SRE (Director)	123. 3	338.87
	PAR (Talkdown)	123. 3	339.97
			344.35
	Tower	122. 1	372.65
	Gnd		311.32
	ATIS		379.75

Key to Abbreviations

1.	AFIS	— Aerodrome Flight Information Service
2.	App	— Approach
3.	ATIS	— Automated Traffic Information Service
4.	CAC	— Centralised Approach Control (Military)
5.	Dep	— Departures
6.	Gnd	— Ground
7.	LARS	— Lower Airspace Radar Service
8.	MAS	— Middle Airspace Service
9.	Ops	— Operations
10.	PAR	— Precision Approach Radar
11.	SRE	— Surveillance Radar Element
12.	VOR	— Very High Frequency Omni Range (Navigation Beacon)

Military airfield frequencies are often referred to by 'stud' numbers, enabling the pilot to select changes of frequency easily and quickly. Stud numbers are given in specialist frequency publications.

Below:
Part of the Jeppesen chart used for transatlantic supersonic flights. *Jeppesen*

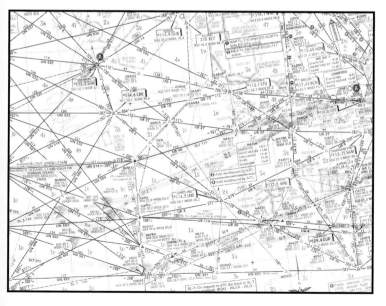

Miscellaneous Frequencies

Emergency   121.500 (V) 243.000 (U)
Military pilots wishing to carry out training
fixes in London airspace use
frequency 245.100.

Shanwick North Atlantic Clearance Delivery
This frequency is used by   127.65
airlines registered east of 30°
West for obtaining clearance
across the North Atlantic.

This frequency is for airlines   123.95
registered west of 30° West
for the same purpose.

This frequency is used at busy   135.525
periods by various airlines, particularly
British Airways, for clearance delivery.

The three frequencies above can be heard in virtually all parts of the United Kingdom.

Fire Services   121.6

Unicom (Scene of Emergency)   130.42

Flight Information Services   127.275 Scottish (West)
                                                        131.300 Scottish (North)
                                                        119.875 Scottish (East)
                                                        125.475 London (North)
                                                        124.600 London (South East)
                                                        124.750 London (South West)

Military Airspace Services   134.300, 249.475 Scottish
                                                        127.450, 231.625 Midlands
                                                        135.150, 275.475 South/South West
                                                        135.275, 299.975 East Anglia/North East

UK Scene of Search and Rescue   244.600

NATO Search and Rescue Training   252.800

NATO International Combined   123.100, 138.700, 282.800
Scene of Search and Rescue

London Joint Area Organisation   231.625 (North West)
                                                        275.350 (Central)
                                                        233.800 (Clacton)
                                                        230.050 (Dover/Lydd)
                                                        251.225 (Seaford/Hurn)
                                                        235.050 (London above FL300)

Appendix III: En-Route Radio Frequencies

The majority of aeronautical radio frequencies for the United Kingdom and Ireland are listed, divided into various geographical regions, together with their operating agencies.

Frequencies are given in six figures. However, note that the sixth digit is not spoken — for example, 126.075 is spoken 'one two six decimal zero seven'. Also, where the fifth digit is zero it is not spoken — for example, 129.600 is spoken 'one two nine decimal six'.

For airport frequencies refer to previous appendix.

Station	Frequencies	
Area 1 — Scotland/North Sea		
123.775	Scottish Control	Primary Frequency
129.225	Scottish Control	Hebrides Upper Control
124.500	Scottish Control	
125.675	Scottish Control	Hebrides Upper Control
133.675	Scottish Control	Hebrides Upper Control
134.775	Scottish Control	
126.300	Scottish Control	
124.820	Scottish Control	
132.720	Scottish Control	
123.375	Scottish Control	TMA via TALLA
126.250	Scottish Control	TMA via GALLOWAY
124.500	Scottish Control	Northern radar service
134.300	Scottish Military	
249.475	Scottish Military	
119.875	Scottish Information	Eastern
127.275	Scottish Information	Western
131.300	Scottish Information	Northern
122.100	Watchdog	Fisheries Protection
123.650	Watchdog	Fisheries Protection
119.250	Sumburgh Radar	
123.150	Sumburgh Radar	
121.250	Aberdeen Radar	
134.100	North Sea Off-Shore Radar Advisory Service	
135.175	Aberdeen Radar	
353.550	Aberdeen Radar	
135.175	Aberdeen Information	
129.950	Viking Approach	East Shetlands Helicopters
122.000	Forties Charlie	Helicopter Routes
122.050	Thistle Alpha	Helicopter Routes
122.450	Claymore Alpha	Helicopter Routes
129.700	Montrose Alpha	Helicopter Routes
129.750	Frigg	Helicopter Routes
Area 2 — Ireland/Isle of Man		
131.050	London Control	Primary Frequency
135.575	London Control	Primary Frequency
126.870	London Control	
129.100	London Control	
134.425	London Control	
125.675	Scottish Control	Primary Frequency
129.225	Scottish Control	Primary Frequency
121.700	Oceanic Clearances	Aircraft on the ground
124.700	Shannon Control	Shannon Sector
127.500	Shannon Control	Cork Sector
131.150	Shannon Control	Cork Sector
132.150	Shannon Control	DEVOL/BABAN Sectors
134.275	Shannon Control	Shannon Sector

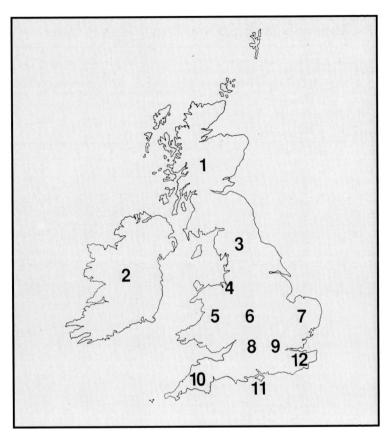

135.225	Shannon Control	Shannon Oceanic Transition Area
135.600	Shannon Control	Shannon Oceanic Transition Area
129.175	Dublin Control	Northern Sector
124.650	Dublin Control	Southern Sector
136.050	Dublin Control	
136.150	Dublin Control	
231.625	Scottish Military	
249.475	Scottish Military	
127.450	Scottish Military	

Area 3 — Northern England

118.775	London Control	Primary Frequency
126.775	London Control	Primary Frequency
131.050	London Control	Primary Frequency
121.325	London Control	
128.125	London Control	
129.100	London Control	

Opposite
The frequency details in this appendix are set out in accordance with the areas shown on this map.

133.525	London Control	
136.200	London Control	
136.275	London Control	
126.650	Manchester Control	FL195 and below
128.675	Pennine Radar	Northern Off-Route Co-ordination Area
125.475	London Information	
127.450	London Military	
135.275	London Military	
231.625	London Military	
299.975	London Military	

Area 4 — North Wales/Manchester

118.775	London Control	Primary Frequency
131.050	London Control	Primary Frequency
135.575	London Control	Primary Frequency
124.200	Manchester Control	FL195 and below
125.950	Manchester Control	FL195 and below
125.100	Manchester Control	FL195 and below
126.650	Manchester Control	FL195 and below
133.050	Manchester Control	FL195 and below
133.400	Manchester Control	FL195 and below
134.925	Manchester Control	FL195 and below
125.475	London Information	
127.450	London Military	
231.625	London Military	

Area 5 — South and Mid-Wales

133.600	London Control	Primary Frequency
129.375	London Control	
136.400	London Control	
135.150	London Military	
275.475	London Military	
124.750	London Information	
135.600	Shannon Control	

Area 6 — Midlands/Birmingham

127.100	London Control	Primary Frequency
130.925	London Control	Primary Frequency
131.125	London Control	Primary Frequency
132.450	London Control	Primary Frequency
118.475	London Control	
127.875	London Control	
128.475	London Control	
129.200	London Control	
132.600	London Control	
133.075	London Control	
133.975	London Control	
124.600	London Information	
127.450	London Military	
135.275	London Military	
231.625	London Military	
275.475	London Military	
299.975	London Military	

Area 7 — East Anglia

129.600	London Control	Primary Frequency
118.475	London Control	Primary Frequency
132.450	London Control	Primary Frequency
133.450	London Control	Primary Frequency

133.525	London Control
136.275	London Control
136.550	London Control
125.275	Anglia Radar
128.925	Anglia Radar
264.575	Anglia Radar
283.475	Anglia Radar
125.750	Amsterdam Control
124.600	London Information
135.275	London Military
233.800	London Military
299.975	London Military

Below:
Long range radar stations for the UK.

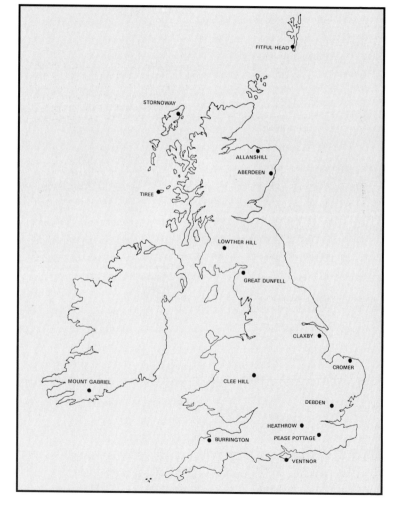

Area 8 — Thames Valley

134.750	London Control	Primary Frequency
133.600	London Control	
136.400	London Control	
126.075	London Control	
135.150	London Military	
275.475	London Military	
124.750	London Information	

Area 9 — Greater London

127.425	London Control	High Level Overflights
135.425	London Control	High Level Overflights
128.425	London Control	
131.125	London Control	
132.450	London Control	
132.600	London Control	
135.325	London Control	
132.700	Thames Radar	
118.825	London Control	)Arrivals and Departures to the London Airports
119.775	London Control	)Arrivals and Departures to the London Airports
120.475	London Control	)Arrivals and Departures to the London Airports
120.525	London Control	)Arrivals and Departures to the London Airports
129.075	London Control	)Arrivals and Departures to the London Airports
235.050	London Military	
275.350	London Military	
124.600	London Information	

Area 10 — Southwest England

126.075	London Control	Primary Frequency
127.700	London Control	Stand-by Frequency
132.950	London Control	
135.250	London Control	
135.150	London Military	
124.750	London Information	
131.175	Brest Control	
133.475	Brest Control	
131.150	Shannon Control	
135.600	Shannon Control	
123.650	Watchdog	Fisheries Protection

Area 11 — Southern England/Isle of Wight

129.425	London Control	Primary Frequency
135.050	London Control	Primary Frequency
135.325	London Control	
120.225	Solent Radar	
125.500	Brest Control	
133.000	Brest Control	
133.475	Brest Control	
134.825	Brest Control	
136.075	Paris Control	
132.000	Paris Control	
132.825	Paris Control	
120.450	Jersey Approach	
125.200	Jersey Approach	
124.750	London Information	
135.150	London Military	
251.225	London Military	
275.350	London Military	
275.475	London Military	

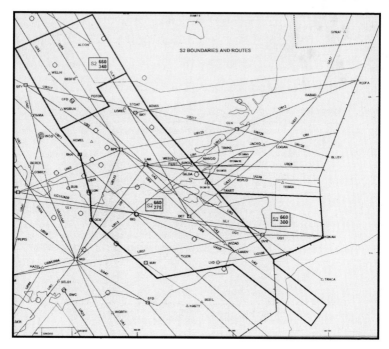

Area 12 — Southeast England

Frequency	Station	Notes
128.425	London Control	Primary Frequency
134.900	London Control	Primary Frequency
132.325	London Control	
132.450	London Control	
135.325	London Control	
135.425	London Control	
136.600	London Control	
132.200	Maastricht Control	
127.625	Maastricht Control	
127.300	Paris Control	
128.275	Paris Control	
131.350	Paris Control	
136.075	Paris Control	
124.750	London Information	
135.150	London Military	
230.050	London Military	
251.225	London Military	

United Kingdom Lower Airspace Radar Service (LARS)

Frequency	Station
126.700	Boscombe Down
128.550	Bristol
134.300	Brize Norton
125.850	Cardiff
125.900	Coltishall
120.800	Coningsby
130.200	Cottesmore

134.050	Culdrose
135.175	Dunsfold
128.150	Exeter
125.250	Farnborough
122.725	Filton
124.675	Humberside
127.750	Leeming
126.500	Leuchars
129.150	Linton-on-Ouse
129.550	London Luton
119.350	Lossiemouth
126.350	Manston
124.150	Marham
124.375	Newcastle
121.250	Plymouth
124.150	Portland
126.500	St Mawgan
120.775	Shawbury
134.350	Valley
127.350	Waddington
124.450	Warton
127.350	Yeovilton

Opposite:
The new S2 sector boundary for southeast England to be operated by the new Swanick Centre. *Civil Aviation Authority*

Below:
The new S3 sector between Trent and Dean Cross which will be operated by the new Swanwick Centre. *Civil Aviation Authority*

United Kingdom Military Middle Airspace Radar Service (MARS)

135.150	London Military	South and West
135.275	London Military	North and East
134.300	Brize Norton	
134.300	Scottish Military	

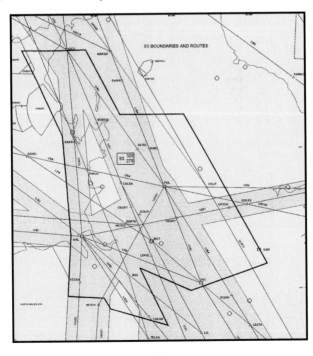

Appendix IV: ICAO Airfield Decode

Four-letter airport decodes in the United Kingdom with a selection of principal airfields in Europe and America.

EG	UNITED KINGDOM	EGHK	Penzance (Heliport)
EGAA	Belfast/Aldergrove	EGHN	Sandown (Isle of Wight)
EGAB	Enniskillen/St Angelo	EGHO	Thruxton
EGAC	Belfast/City	EGHR	Chichester/Goodwood
EGAE	Londonderry/Eglinton	EGJA	Alderney
EGBB	Birmingham	EGJB	Guernsey
EGBD	Derby	EGJJ	Jersey
EGBE	Coventry	EGKA	Shoreham
EGBG	Leicester	EGKB	Biggin Hill
EGBJ	Gloucestershire	EGKH	Lashenden/Headcorn
EGBK	Northampton/Sywell	EGKK	London/Gatwick
EGBM	Tatenhill	EGKR	Redhill
EGBN	Nottingham	EGLA	Bodmin
EGBO	Halfpenny Green	EGLC	London/City
EGBP	Pailton	EGLD	Denham
EGBS	Shobdon	EGLF	Farnborough (Civ)
EGBW	Wellesbourne Mountford	EGLK	Blackbushe
EGCB	Manchester/Barton	EGLL	London/Heathrow
EGCC	Manchester	EGLM	White Waltham
EGCD	Woodford	EGLS	Old Sarum
EGCF	Sandtoft	EGLW	London (Westland Heliport)
EGCG	Strubby (Heliport)	EGMC	Southend
EGCH	Holyhead (Heliport)	EGMD	Lydd
EGCI	Doncaster	EGMH	Manston (Civ)
EGCJ	Sherburn-in-Elmet	EGNB	Brough
EGCK	Caernarfon	EGNC	Carlisle
EGCL	Fenland	EGNF	Nether Thorpe
EGCS	Sturgate	EGNH	Blackpool
EGDA	Brawdy	EGNI	Skegness/Ingoldmells
EGDC	Chivenor	EGNJ	Humberside
EGDG	St Mawgan	EGNL	Barrow/Walney Island
EGDJ	Upavon	EGNM	Leeds/Bradford
EGDL	Lyneham	EGNO	Warton
EGDM	Boscombe Down	EGNR	Hawarden
EGDN	Netheravon	EGNS	Isle of Man/Ronaldsway
EGDR	Culdrose	EGNT	Newcastle
EGDT	Wroughton	EGNV	Teesside
EGDX	St Athan	EGNW	Wickenby
EGDY	Yeovilton	EGNX	East Midlands
EGFC	Cardiff (Heliport)	EGOD	Llanbedr
EGFE	Haverfordwest	EGOE	Ternhill
EGFF	Cardiff	EGOQ	Mona
EGFH	Swansea	EGOS	Shawbury
EGGD	Bristol	EGOV	Valley
EGGP	Liverpool	EGOW	Woodvale
EGGW	Luton	EGOY	West Freugh
EGHA	Compton Abbas	EGPA	Kirkwall
EGHC	Land's End/St Just	EGPB	Sumburgh
EGHD	Plymouth	EGPC	Wick
EGHE	Scilly Isles/St Marys	EGPD	Aberdeen/Dyce
EGHG	Yeovil	EGPE	Inverness
EGHH	Bournemouth	EGPF	Glasgow
EGHI	Southampton/Eastleigh	EGPG	Cumbernauld
EGHJ	Bembridge (Isle of Wight)	EGPH	Edinburgh

EGPI	Islay	EGSS	London/Stansted
EGPJ	Fife/Glenrothes	EGSU	Duxford
EGPK	Prestwick (Civ)	EGSY	Sheffield City
EGPL	Benbecula	EGTB	Wycombe Air Park/Booker
EGPM	Scatsta	EGTC	Cranfield
EGPN	Dundee	EGTD	Dunsfold
EGPO	Stornoway	EGTE	Exeter
EGPR	Barra	EGTF	Fairoaks
EGPT	Perth/Scone	EGTG	Filton
EGPU	Tiree	EGTK	Oxford/Kidlington
EGPW	Unst	EGTO	Rochester
EGPY	Dounreay/Thurso	EGTR	Elstree
EGQJ	Machrihanish	EGUB	Benson
EGQK	Kinloss	EGUC	Aberporth
EGQL	Leuchars	EGUF	Farnborough (Mil)
EGQM	Boulmer	EGUH	High Wycombe
EGQR	Saxa Vord	EGUL	Lakenheath
EGQS	Lossiemouth	EGUM	Manston (Mil)
EGQT	Edinburgh Turnhouse (Mil)	EGUN	Mildenhall
EGSB	Bedford (Castle Mill)	EGUO	Colerne
EGSC	Cambridge	EGUP	Sculthorpe
EGSD	Great Yarmouth (North Denes)	EGUS	Lee-on-Solent
EGSE	Ipswich	EGUY	Wyton
EGSF	Peterborough/Conington	EGVA	Fairford
EGSG	Stapleford	EGVN	Brize Norton
EGSH	Norwich	EGVO	Odiham
EGSJ	Seething	EGVP	Middle Wallop
EGSL	Andrewsfield		
EGSM	Beccles (Heliport)		
EGSO	Crowfield		
EGSP	Peterborough/Sibson		

Below:
High level routes over Northern France.
Eurocontrol

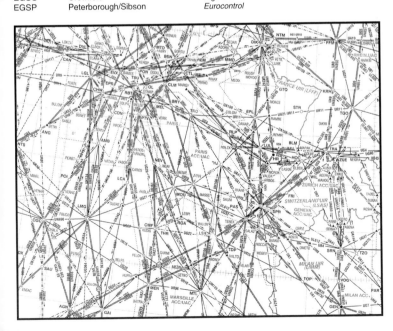

EGWC	Cosford
EGWN	Halton
EGWU	Northolt
EGXC	Coningsby
EGXD	Dishforth
EGXE	Leeming
EGXG	Church Fenton
EGXJ	Cottesmore
EGXN	Newton
EGXT	Wittering
EGXU	Linton-on-Ouse
EGXW	Waddington
EGXZ	Topcliffe
EGYC	Coltishall
EGYD	Cranwell
EGYE	Barkston Heath
EGYM	Marham
EGYP	Mount Pleasant
BI	**ICELAND**
BIKF	Keflavik
BIRK	Reykjavik
CY	**CANADA**
CYAY	St Anthony
CYEG	Edmonton
CYHZ	Halifax
CYMX	Montreal/Mirabel
CYOW	Ottawa
CYQB	Quebec
CYQM	Moncton
CYQX	Gander
CYVR	Vancouver
CYWG	Winnipeg
CYXD	Edmonton
CYYC	Calgary
CYYR	Goose
CYYT	St Johns
CYYZ	Toronto
EB	**BELGIUM**
EBAW	Antwerp
EBBR	Brussels
EBOS	Ostend
ED	**GERMANY**
EDAF	Rhein Main
EDDF	Frankfurt Main
EDDH	Hamburg
EDDI	Berlin (Tempelhof)
EDDK	Cologne Bonn
EDDL	Düsseldorf
EDDM	Munich
EDDN	Nürnberg
EDDS	Stuttgart
EDDT	Berlin (Tegel)
EDDV	Hanover
EDDW	Bremen
EDLE	Essen/Mulheim
EDLG	Münster/Osnabrück
EDRS	Saarbrücken
EF	**FINLAND**

EFHF	Helsinki (Malmi)
EFHK	Helsinki (Vantaa)
EH	**NETHERLANDS**
EHAM	Amsterdam/Schiphol
EHBK	Maastricht
EHEH	Eindhoven
EHRD	Rotterdam
EI	**IRELAND**
EICK	Cork
EIDW	Dublin
EIKN	Connaught
EIKY	Kerry/Farranfore
EIME	Baldonnel/Casement
EINN	Shannon
EISG	Sligo
EIWF	Waterford
EK	**DENMARK**
EKCH	Copenhagen/Kastrup
EKEB	Esbjerg
EKRK	Copenhagen/Roskilde
EL	**LUXEMBOURG**
ELLX	Luxembourg
EN	**NORWAY**
ENBO	Bodo
ENBR	Bergen/Flesland
ENCN	Kristiansand/Kjevik
ENFB	Oslo/Fornebu
ENGM	Oslo/Gardemoen
ENKB	Kristiansund/Kvernberget
ENVA	Trondheim/Vaernes
ENZV	Stavanger/Sola
EP	**POLAND**
EPGD	Gdansk/Rebiechowo
EPWA	Warsaw/Okecie
ES	**SWEDEN**
ESCN	Stockholm/Tullinge
ESKN	Stockholm/Skavsta
ESMS	Malmo/Sturup
ESSA	Stockholm/Arlanda
ESSB	Stockholm/Bromma
ET	**GERMANY**
ETBS	Berlin/Schönefeld
ETAR	Ramstein
ETNB	Berlin/Tegel
ETHH	Bonn
ETUL	Laarbruch
ETUO	Gütersloh
ETUR	Bruggen
EV	**LATVIA**
EVRA	Riga

GC	CANARY ISLANDS
GCLP	Las Palmas De Gran Canaria
GCRR	Lanzarote
GCTS	Tenerife Sur/Reina Sofia
GCXO	Tenerife/Santa Cruz

KA-KW	UNITED STATES
KABQ	Albuquerque Intl, NM
KADW	Andrews AFB, Md
KAEX	England AFB, La
KATL	Atlanta Intl, FA
KBFI	Seattle (Boeing Field), Wa
KBGR	Bangor Intl, Me
KBOS	Boston Logan, Ma
KBWI	Baltimore-Washington Intl, Md
KCHS	Charleston AFB, SC
KCVS	Cannon AFB, NM
KDOV	Dover AFB, De
KEDW	Edwards AFB, Ca
KELP	El Paso Intl, Tx
KEWR	Newark Intl, NJ
KEYW	Key West Intl, Fl
KFLL	Fort Lauderdale, Fl
KFMH	Otis AFB, Ma
KFOE	Forbes AFB, Ks
KFWH	Carswell AFB, Tx
KGFA	Malmstrom AFB, Mt
KGFK	Grand Forks Intl, ND
KGTF	Great Falls Intl, Mt
KGUS	Grissom AFB, In
KGVW	Richards-Gebaur AFB, Mo
KHMN	Holloman AFB, NM
KHOU	Houston, Tx
KHST	Homestead AFB, Fl
KIAB	McConnell AFB, Ks
KIAD	Washington/Dulles, DC
KIAG	Niagara Falls Intl, NY
KIAH	Houston International, Tx
KIND	Indianapolis Intl, In
KJAX	Jacksonville Intl, Fl
KJFK	John F. Kennedy Intl, NY
KLAX	Los Angeles Intl, Ca
KLFI	Langley AFB, Va
KLGA	La Guardia, NY
KLRF	Little Rock AFB, Ar
KLVS	Las Vegas, Nv
KMCI	Kansas City Intl, Mo
KMEM	Memphis Intl, Tn
KMIA	Miami Intl, Fl
KMSP	Minneapolis-St Paul Intl, Mn
KMSY	New Orleans, La
KNBG	New Orleans NAS, La
KNIP	Jacksonville NAS, Fl
KNSF	Andrews AFB/NAF Washington, Md
KONT	Ontario Intl, Ca
KORD	Chicago O'Hare, Il
KPDX	Portland Intl, Or
KPHL	Philadelphia Intl, Pa
KPIT	Pittsburgh, Pe
KPOB	Pope AFB, NC
KPSM	Pease AFB, NH

KRCA	Ellsworth AFB, SD
KRIC	Richmond International, Va
KRNO	Reno Intl, Nv
KSAN	San Diego Intl, Ca
KSAT	San Antonio Intl, Tx
KSEA	Seattle, Wa
KSFO	San Francisco Intl, Ca
KSKF	Kelly AFB, Wa
KSLC	Salt Lake City Intl, Ut
KSTL	St Louis Intl, Mo
KTPA	Tampa Intl, Fl
KTUL	Tulsa Intl, Ok
KVAD	Moody AFB, Ga
KWRI	McGuire AFB, NJ
KYIP	Detroit, Mi

LB	BULGARIA
LBBG	Burgas
LBSF	Sofia
LBWN	Varna

LC	CYPRUS
LCLK	Larnaca
LCPH	Paphos Intl
LCRA	Akrotiri
LCRR	Nicosia (Mil)

LD	CROATIA
LDDU	Dubrovnik
LDSP	Split
LDZA	Zagreb

LE	SPAIN
LEAL	Alicante
LEAS	Asturias
LEBB	Bilbao
LEBL	Barcelona
LEGE	Gerona
LEGR	Granada
LEIB	Ibiza
LEMD	Madrid/Barajas
LEMG	Malaga
LEMH	Isla De Menorca/Menorca
LEPA	Palma De Mallorca
LESO	San Sebastian
LEST	Santiago
LETO	Madrid/Torrejon De Ardoz
LEVC	Valencia
LEXJ	Santander
LEZL	Seville

LF	FRANCE
LFAT	Le Touquet/Paris Plage
LFBD	Bordeaux/Merignac
LFBF	Toulouse/Francazal
LFLF	Orléans
LFMN	Nice/Côte D'Azur
LFMP	Perpignan/Rivesaltes
LFMT	Montpellier/Frejorques
LFPB	Paris/Le Bourget
LFPG	Paris/Charles De Gaulle
LFPO	Paris/Orly

LFSB	Basle/Mulhouse	**LS**	**SWITZERLAND**
LFSD	Dijon/Longvic	LSGG	Geneva/Cointrin
LFST	Strasbourg/Entzheim	LSGL	Lausanne
		LSGZ	Zermatt
LG	**GREECE**	LSMB	Berne
LGAT	Athens Intl	LSXM	St Moritz
LGEL	Athens/Elefsis	LSZB	Berne/Belp
LGZA	Zakinthos	LSZH	Zurich
LH	**HUNGARY**	**LT**	**TURKEY**
LHBP	Budapest/Ferihegy	LTAC	Ankara/Esenboga
		LTAD	Ankara/Etimesgut
LI	**ITALY**	LTAE	Ankara/Akinci
LIMC	Milan/Malpensa	LTBA	Istanbul/Atatürk
LIMF	Turin/Caselle	LTBU	Corfu
LIML	Milan/Linate	LTBJ	Izmir/Adnan Menderes Intl
LIPX	Verona/Villafranca	LTBL	Izmir/Cigli
LIPZ	Venice/Tessera		
LIRA	Rome/Ciampino	**LW**	**MACEDONIA**
LIRF	Rome/Fiumicino	LWSK	Skopje
LIRN	Naples/Capodichino		
LIRP	Pisa/San Giusto	**LX**	**GIBRALTAR**
LIRQ	Florence	LXGB	Gibraltar
LJ	**SLOVENIA**	**LY**	**YUGOSLAVIA**
LJLJ	Ljubljana	LYBE	Belgrade
LJMB	Maribor		
LJPZ	Potoroz	**LZ**	**SLOVAKIA**
		LZIB	Bratislava
LK	**CZECH REPUBLIC**		
LKPR	Prague/Ruzyne	**OA**	**AFGHANISTAN**
		OAKB	Kabul
LL	**ISRAEL**		
LLBG	Tel Aviv/Ben Gurion	**OB**	**BAHRAIN**
LLJR	Jerusalem	OBBI	Bahrain/International
LM	**MALTA**	**OE**	**SAUDI ARABIA**
LMML	Luqa	OEDR	Dhahran Intl
		OEJN	Jeddah/King Abdul Aziz Intl
LO	**AUSTRIA**	OERK	Riyadh/King Khalid Intl
LOWI	Innsbruck	OERY	Riyadh
LOWK	Klagenfurt		
LOWS	Salzburg	**OI**	**IRAN**
LOWW	Vienna/Schwechat	OIID	Tehran/Doshan Tappeh
		OIIG	Tehran/Ghale Morghi
LP	**PORTUGAL**	OIII	Tehran/Mehrabad Intl
	(MADEIRA AND AZORES)	OISS	Shiraz Intl
LPAZ	Santa Maria	OIZH	Zahedan Int
LPFL	Flores		
LPFU	Funchal	**OJ**	**JORDAN**
LPLA	Lajes	OJAI	Amman/Queen Alia Intl
LPPD	Ponta Delgada	OJJO	Jericho
LPPR	Porto		
LPPT	Lisbon	**OK**	**KUWAIT**
		OKAF	Kuwait Military
LQ	**BOSNIA AND HERZEGOVINA**	OKBK	Kuwait Intl
LQSA	Sarajevo		
		OL	**LEBANON**
LR	**ROMANIA**	OLBA	Beirut Intl
LRBS	Bucharest/Baneasa		
LROP	Bucharest/Otopeni	**OM**	**UNITED ARAB EMIRATEs**
		OMAA	Abu Dhabi Intl

OMDB	Dubai Intl	**PA**	**ALASKA**	
OMFJ	Fujairah Intl	PANC	Anchorage Intl	
OMSJ	Sharjah Intl	PAFA	Fairbanks Intl	
OO	**OMAN**			
OOMS	Muscat/Seeb Intl	**SF**	**FALKLAND ISLANDS**	
		SFAL	Stanley	
OP	**PAKISTAN**			
OPKC	Karachi Intl	**TX**	**BERMUDA**	
OPKD	Hyderabad	TXKF	Bermuda	
OPLA	Lahore			
OPRN	Islamabad/Chaklala	**UL/UU**	**RUSSIA**	
OPSF	Karachi/Sharea Faisal	ULLI	Saint Petersburg/Pulkovo	
		UUEE	Moscow/Sheremetyevo	
OR	**IRAQ**	UUMM	Murmansk	
ORBS	Baghdad/Saddam Intl	UUWW	Moscow/Vnukovo	
ORMM	Basrah			
ORNW	Baghdad/Muthenne	**UK**	**UKRAINE/MOLDAVIA**	
		UKBB	Kiev	
OS	**SYRIA**	UKOO	Odessa	
OSDI	Damascus Intl			
		UL	**ESTONIA**	
OT	**QATAR**	ULTT	Tallinn	
OTBD	Doha Intl			

Below:
Manchester Air Traffic Control Centre.
Civil Aviation Authority

OY **YEMEN REPUBLIC**
OYAA Aden Acc/Aden Intl

Appendix V: ATC Reporting Points and Radio Navigation Aids

Modern navigation relies on a combination of radio beacons and reporting points at airway intersections and airspace boundaries. Aircraft positions are determined by on-board inertial navigation systems as well as radio signals from VHF beacons.

The following lists cover UK five-letter reporting points, followed by radio navigation facilities, with a selection from adjoining regions.

The first list covers five-letter reporting points. These are navigation positions, none of which have a radio transmitter on the ground. They are invariably at airway or upper air route intersections or on national airspace boundaries.

The name of the facility is followed by the co-ordinates, and the third column indicates its purpose.

Ident	Co-ordinates	Location
ABDAL	N5127 W0150	Bristol/Cardiff Arrivals
ABSIL	N5438 E0420	UA37
ACORN	N5114 E0011	LTMA — Gatwick SIDs
ADMIS	N5160 E0011	UB317 and UR77
ADSON	N5103 W0215	R37
AGANO	N4939 W0200	Channel Islands CTR — Alderney Arrivals
AKELO	N4946 W0353	SL1 — SL4 — SL7
ALICE	N5817 W0250	Aberdeen/Atlantic Rim
ALKIN	N5123 E0011	LTMA — London City and Biggin Hill STARs
ALLOY	N6121 E0147	East Shetland
ALVIN	N5139 W0240	G1
ALWYN	N6048 E0144	East Shetland
AMLET	N5316 W0150	Manchester TMA
AMMAN	N5150 W0359	G1
ANGEL	N5447 E0308	UL74 — UR4
ANGLA	N4942 W0201	Channel Islands CTR
ANGLO	N4956 W0027	Jersey/Guernsey Arrivals
ANGUS	N5641 W0303	B2 — B226
ANNET	N4939 W0400	UL722 — UR116
APPLE	N5430 W0231	UN590
ARTHA	N5347 W0217	Manchester/Liverpool Arrivals
ASKEY/LOREL	N5200 W0003	Stansted and Luton STARs
ASKIL	N4903 W0700	UT7 Brest Boundary
ASPEN	N5017 W0148	UR24 — UR41
ASPIT	N5622 W0500	UN582
ASTRA	N5051 W0008	LTMA — Gatwick STARs
ATWEL	N5630 E0033	UN581
AVANT	N5049 W0056	Gatwick Arrivals
BADGA	N5154 E0016	M604 — Y4 — UM604 — UY4
BAGIN	N5102 E0135	UG106 — Gatwick STARs
BAKER	N5129 E0018	B4 — LTMA
BAKUR	N5215 W0538	UA29 — UN546
BALIS	N5714 W0203	Aberdeen ATSU
BAMES	N4858 E0129	UA1 (near Paris CDG)
BANBA	N5157 W0614	UB10 — UR72 Shannon Boundary
BANDU	N5029 W1008	Shannon Oceanic Transition
BANLO	N5100 W0800	Shannon Oceanic Transition
BARIX	N5025 W0800	Shannon Oceanic Transition
BARLU	N4941 W0118	UB11 Brest Control
BARTN	N5328 W0225	Manchester TMA

Ident	Co-ordinates	Location
BASAV	N5206 E0206	UA37 — UR77
BASET	N5133 W0142	UB39 — UG1
BATEL	N5053 E0033	LTMA
BATSU	N5555 E0500	UN611
BEDFO	N5213 W0033	B4 — UB4
BEECH	N5028 E0012	G27 — London City and Biggin Hill STARs
BEENO	N5312 E0302	B5 — UA37 — UB5
BEGAS	N4500 W0900	Shannon Oceanic Transition
BEGDA	N5236 W0402	UB39 — UW502
BEGTO	N5046 W0114	H51 — R84 — Heathrow Arrivals
BEKET	N5853 W0131	W5D
BENBO	N5027 E0000	A1 — A56 — UA1
BENDY	N5017 W0148	Southampton CTA
BENIX	N4932 W0129	Channel Islands CTR
BENTY	N5946 W0108	Sumburgh Heli Routes
BEREK	N5139 W0105	A1 — LTMA — Gatwick STARs
BESOP	N5433 W0527	UB2 — UP6
BEVAV	N4904 W0141	Channel Islands Arrivals
BEWLI	N5046 W0148	H51 — Heathrow/Gatwick Arrivals
BEXIL	N5042 E0044	En route Hold — Gatwick STARs
BILLY	N6001 W0083	UN603 — UN610 — Hebrides UTA
BIRCH	N5224 W0155	Birmingham CTR and CTA
BISKI	N4906 W0800	Shannon Oceanic Transition
BLACA	N5453 W0509	B2 — Edinburgh — Glasgow STARs
BLUFA	N5256 E0309	B1 — UB1 — UB105
BLUSY	N5137 E0209	R126 — Heathrow STARs — UR126
BODAM	N5955 W0116	Sumburgh Heli Routes
BOGNA	N5042 W0015	A1 — Heathrow/Gatwick SIDs
BOLTA	N5449 E0041	UW550
BONBY	N5753 W0420	W3D -Inverness
BONDY	N5107 E0045	LTMA — London City and Biggin Hill STARs
BORMA	N5751 W0325	UN582 — UN611
BORVE	N5748 W0228	Aberdeen/Atlantic Rim
BOVVA	N5143 W0032	LTMA — Heathrow STARs
BOWES	N5431 W0206	Northern Radar Advisory Area
BOYNE	N5346 W0530	W911D
BOYSI	N5159 E0003	Luton/Stansted Arrivals
BRAIN	N5148 E0039	R123 — London City and Biggin Hill STARs
BRASO	N5141 E0041	R1 — LTMA — Heathrow, Stansted and Luton STARs
BREKI	N6232 W1932	Iceland UIR
BRILL	N4942 W0223	Channel Islands CTR
BRIPO	N5042 W0245	R8
BRUCE	N5614 W0550	N573D — W958D
BRYNA	N5151 W0351	UW502
BUKLI	N5000 W0025	Y91 — -UY91
BUNCE	N5132 W0024	Y3 — UP2
BUKEN	N5420 W0206	Manchester/Liverpool SIDs
BURAK	N5300 W1200	Shannon UIR
BURNI	N5344 W0231	Manchester/Liverpool Arrivals
BUSTA	N5205 E0004	LTMA — Stansted and Luton STARs
BUZAD	N5156 W0033	A20 — B3 — Heathrow/Northolt/Stansted SIDs
CALDA	N5346 W0238	A1 — UA1 — Manchester TMA
CAMBO	N4917 W0551	UR72 Brest Boundary
CARBO	N6055 E0015	East Shetland Basin
CASEL	N5349 W0410	B3 — Isle of Man Arrivals
CAVAL	N4929 W0452	UR168
CEDAR	N5231 W0149	Birmingham CTA
CELLO	N6214 W2028	Iceland UIR
CHANL	N5027 E0010	Gatwick Hold

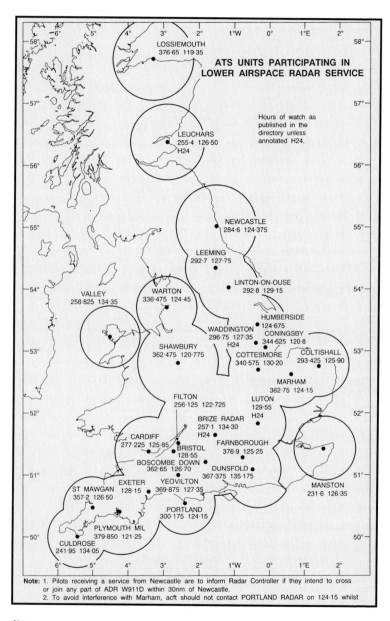

ATS UNITS PARTICIPATING IN
LOWER AIRSPACE RADAR SERVICE

Hours of watch as
published in the
directory unless
annotated H24.

LOSSIEMOUTH
376·65 119·35

LEUCHARS
255·4 126·50
H24

NEWCASTLE
284·6 124·375

LEEMING
292·7 127·75

LINTON-ON-OUSE
292·8 129·15

VALLEY
258·825 134·35

WARTON
336·475 124·45

HUMBERSIDE
124·675

WADDINGTON
296·75 127·35
H24

CONINGSBY
344·625 120·8

SHAWBURY
362·475 120·775

COTTESMORE
340·575 130·20

COLTISHALL
293·425 125·90

MARHAM
362·75 124·15

FILTON
256·125 122·725

LUTON
129·55
H24

BRIZE RADAR
257·1 134·30
H24

CARDIFF
277·225 125·85

BRISTOL
128·55

FARNBOROUGH
376·9 125·25

BOSCOMBE DOWN
362·65 126·70

DUNSFOLD
367·375 135·175

ST MAWGAN
357·2 126·50

EXETER
128·15

YEOVILTON
369·875 127·35

MANSTON
231·6 126·35

PORTLAND
300·175 124·15

PLYMOUTH MIL
379·850 121·25

CULDROSE
241·95 134·05

Note: 1. Pilots receiving a service from Newcastle are to inform Radar Controller if they intend to cross
or join any part of ADR W911D within 30nm of Newcastle.
2. To avoid interference with Marham, acft should not contact PORTLAND RADAR on 124·15 whilst

Above:
Coverage of the lower Airspace Radar Service. *Royal Air Force*

Ident	Co-ordinates	Location
CHASE	N5236 W0154	Birmingham Arrivals
CHELT	N5152 W0222	B39 — UA251 — UB39
CHINN	N5757 W0411	W3D
CHUBB	N4925 W0248	Jersey Arrivals and SIDs
CLIFF	N5052 E0043	A20 — Heathrow STARs — UA20
CLIPY	N5200 W0011	London City/Biggin Hill/Luton/Stansted Arrivals
CLYDE	N5557 W0447	Glasgow STARs and SIDs — Scottish TMA — W910D
CODEY	N5119 W0132	Farnborough Arrivals
COLRE	N5507 W0644	Londonderry/Eglinton
CONGA	N5308 W0211	A1 — R101 — Manchester TMA — Manchester SIDs
COWLY	N5137 W0103	A1 — R41 — UA1 — UR41
CRABE	N5102 E0014	UG106
CREWE	N5249 W0218	UA251
CROFT	N5336 W0231	Manchester TMA
CUMBO	N5556 W0357	Edinburgh SIDs — Scottish TMA
CUMRI	N5143 W0260	UN862
CUTEL	N5553 E0022	UL7 — UL983
DAGGA	N5149 E0005	R123/Gatwick Departures
DALEY/ROSUN	N5340 W0221	Manchester/Liverpool Arrivals
DALKY	N5359 W0554	B2 — UB2 — Belfast TMA
DANDI	N5520 E0500	UL975 — UM604 — UN866 — UW550
DAVOT	N5720 W0405	En route Hold (Advisory Routes) — W3D
DAWLY	N5034 W0327	R8 — UA25 — UA29
DAYNE	N5314 W0202	Manchester Arrivals
DEGOS	N5411 W0654	UN517
DELBO	N5152 W0012	Gatwick Arrivals
DENBY	N5331 W0157	Manchester CTR
DEVAL	N5051 E0013	A2 — UA2 — UB4 — UL613
DEPSO	N6055 E0152	East Shetland Basin
DIDEL	N5051 W0400	UA29 — UL3
DIKAS	N5146 W0315	UA25 — UB40 — UG1
DOGGA	N5323 E0155	B1 — B5 — UB1 — UB5
DOLIP	N5200 W1200	Shannon UIR
DONNA	N5142 W0044	Heathrow Arrivals
DORKI	N5116 W0002	Heathrow Arrivals (Hold)
DOWNI	N5704 W0206	Aberdeen Holding Fix
DRAKE	N5012 W0004	A34 — A56 — R25 — UA34
DUFFY	N5430 W0551	Belfast TMA
DUMBA	N5556 W0433	Glasgow SIDs — Scottish TMA
DUNLO	N5458 W0642	UN570 — UP6
EAGLE	N5124 E0005	Biggin Hill
EASIN	N5339 E0007	Southern North Sea Area
EBONY	N5220 W0203	Birmingham CTR and CTA
EIDER	N6121 E0109	East Shetland Basin
ELDER	N5039 W0120	Heathrow and Gatwick STARs
ELDIN	N5309 E0321	B5 — UB5
ELGAR	N5223 W0256	UN862
EMJEE	N5423 E0153	UW534
ERING	N5135 E0136	B29 — UB29
ERMIN	N5020 W0355	Plymouth
ERNAN	N5416 W0723	UN550 — UN560
ERWAN	N4556 W0512	UR107 Brest Control
ESKDO	N5517 W0312	B4 — Edinburgh STARs
ESTRY	N5340 W0316	Manchester/Warton/Blackpool
ETIKI	N4800 W0085	Brest Oceanic Transition
ETRAT	N4941 E0009	A34 France Control
EVRIN	N5146 W0634	UL607 Shannon Boundary
EXMOR	N5110 W0321	UA25 — UA251 — UR14 — UR37

Ident	Co-ordinates	Location
FAMBO	N5430 W0027	UB5
FAWBO	N5000 W0119	B11 — UB11
FENIK	N5543 W0417	UA1 — UB2 Scottish TMA
FERAS	N5138 E0038	London TMA
FERIT	N5138 E0032	UB29 — UM14
FILET	N5551 E0033	UL983
FIMLI	N5118 W0004	Heathrow Arrivals
FINCH	N5133 W0010	A20
FINDO	N5622 W0327	UB2 — UB4 — UR38
FINMA	N5160 W0103	A47 — B71
FIWUD	N5352 W0304	Leeds/Bradford Departures
FLAME	N6102 E0155	East Shetland Basin
FLARE	N6102 E0015	East Shetland Basin
FORTY	N5757 E0035	UB2 — UL7
FOYLE	N5608 W0422	Glasgow STARs and SIDs
FRANK	N5142 W0041	LTMA — Northolt SIDs
FULMA	N5530 W0500	Scottish TMA — W958D
FYNER	N5602 W0506	Glasgow Arrivals
GABAD	N5201 E0203	Stansted/Luton Arrivals
GAPLI	N5000 W0800	Shannon Oceanic Transition
GARVA	N5741 W0430	W6D
GASKO	N5413 W0016	Northern Off-Route Area
GAVEL	N5923 W0124	W5D
GELKI	N5360 W0554	Belfast Terminal Area
GIBSO	N5045 W0230	R8 — UR8 — UR14
GILDA	N5136 E0035	UG39 — UR12
GILOK	N5527 W0043	Prestwick Approach
GINIS	N5327 W0045	B1 — UB1
GIPER	N5100 W1200	Shannon Oceanic Transition
GIRDO	N5547 E0050	UL983
GIRNU	N6028 W0004	Scatsta Approaches
GIRVA	N5511 W0453	Edinburgh and Glasgow STARs
GLESK	N5654 W0247	B2
GODAL	N5116 W0044	Gatwick Arrivals
GOLES	N5336 W0104	UB1—UB105
GONUT	N6100 W0435	UH70
GORSE	N5710 W0153	Aberdeen Heli Routes
GRICE	N5611 W0341	Edinburgh STARs and SIDs — Glasgow STARs
GULDA	N4923 W0155	Jersey Departures
GUNPA	N6100 0000	UP19 — UP610
GUNSO	N4904 W1144	Shannon Oceanic Transition
HALIF	N5344 W0135	UL613 — UN590 — UR4
HANKY	N5107 W0108	London Terminal Area/Pepis
HARDY	N5028 E0029	A47 — Heathrow SIDs — UA47 — Gatwick SIDs
HASTY	N5043 E0032	G27
HAWKE	N5022 E0006	A1 — G27 — UA1 — UG27
HAYDO	N5328 W0233	UP6 Radar Vectoring Point
HAZEL	N5100 W0058	Heathrow, Stansted and Luton STARs
HEIDI	N5206 W0037	A2 — B317
HELEN	N5114 E0352	UB29 Brussels
HEMEL	N5148 W0025	UA20 — UH52 — UH53 — UH54
HERON	N5520 W0500	Scottish TMA — N552D — N562D
HILLY	N5120 E0015	Heathrow Arrivals
HOGBA	N5113 W0003	Heathrow Arrivals
HOLLY	N5053 W0005	Gatwick Arrivals

Below:
The regions of the United Kingdom used for setting altimeters according to barometric pressure.
Royal Air Force

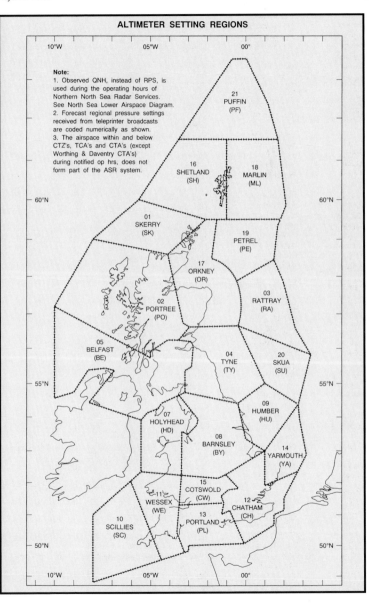

ALTIMETER SETTING REGIONS

Note:
1. Observed QNH, instead of RPS, is used during the operating hours of Northern North Sea Radar Services. See North Sea Lower Airspace Diagram.
2. Forecast regional pressure settings received from teleprinter broadcasts are coded numerically as shown.
3. The airspace within and below CTZ's, TCA's and CTA's (except Worthing & Daventry CTA's) during notified op hrs, does not form part of the ASR system.

21 PUFFIN (PF)

16 SHETLAND (SH)

18 MARLIN (ML)

01 SKERRY (SK)

19 PETREL (PE)

17 ORKNEY (OR)

03 RATTRAY (RA)

02 PORTREE (PO)

05 BELFAST (BE)

04 TYNE (TY)

20 SKUA (SU)

09 HUMBER (HU)

07 HOLYHEAD (HD)

08 BARNSLEY (BY)

14 YARMOUTH (YA)

15 COTSWOLD (CW)

11 WESSEX (WE)

12 CHATHAM (CH)

10 SCILLIES (SC)

13 PORTLAND (PL)

10°W   05°W   00°

60°N   60°N
55°N   55°N
50°N   50°N

Ident	Co-ordinates	Location
INLAK	N5128 W0131	UB29 — UB39 — UL607
IZACK	N5953 W0101	Sumburgh Heli Routes
JACKO	N5144 E0125	B317 — R1
KARIL	N4919 W0152	Channel Islands CTR — Jersey Arrivals and SIDs
KARNO	N5253 W0254	N862 — UN862
KATHY	N5031 W0119	B11 — UB11 — Gatwick STARs
KELLY	N5354 W0421	B3 — Isle of Man Arrivals
KENET	N5131 W0127	G1 — Heathrow, Gatwick, Stansted and Luton STARs
KENUK	N5000 W1200	Shannon Oceanic Transition
KESON	N5232 E0014	UN866
KETIK	N4919 W0152	Jersey Departures
KIDLI	N5146 W0122	A34 — B321 — UA34 — UB321
KINDR	N5323 W0156	Woodford Arrivals
KIPPA	N5310 E0143	UB105
KIRBY	N5328 W0252	Manchester TMA
KISTA	N5930 W0156	En route Hold W3D
KLONN	N5823 E0249	P600D — UP600
KOKAL	N5857 W0253	W3D
KOLEY	N5448 E0313	UL7 — UL975
KOMIK	N5259 E0251	UL603 — UM604 — UN866
KOMOK	N5526 W0041	Prestwick Approach
KONAN	N5107 E0200	UG1 — UL1
KORAK	N5323 W0746	Shannon UIR
KORIB	N5413 W1300	North Atlantic Entry Point
KORUL	N4450 W0655	Brest/Madrid Boundary
KURAD	N5049 W0033	UW502 — UY91
LAGER	N5336 W0008	Southern North Sea HMR 9
LAKEY	N5414 W0009	Manchester/Liverpool Arrivals
LAMMA	N5551 W0245	UR38
LANAK	N5542 W0355	Glasgow STARs — Scottish TMA
LAPEX	N4700 W0080	Brest Oceanic Transition
LARCK	N5054 E0027	Gatwick STARs
LASNO	N4835 W0900	Shannon Oceanic Transition
LECKI	N5528 W0042	Prestwick Approach
LERAK	N4902 W0225	Channel Islands CTR
LESTA	N5244 W0104	B4 — UB4 — UP6
LIBBA	N5543 W0345	Edinburgh/Glasgow Arrivals
LIFFY	N5328 W0530	B1 — UB1
LINDY	N5128 W0102	UA34 — UG1
LIRKI	N6100 W0151	UH71
LISBO	N5431 W0605	Belfast TMA
LIZAD	N4935 W0420	Jersey SIDs — UG4 — UR40 — G4D
LOGAN	N5144 E0136	A37 — R1 — R126 — Heathrow, London City, Biggin Hill, Stansted and Luton STARs
LOMON	N5603 W0434	Scottish TMA — Glasgow STARs and SIDs
LONAM	N5350 E0356	UL7
LOREL/ASKEY	N5200 W0003	LTMA — Stansted and Luton STARs
LOTEE	N4439 W0550	Brest/Madrid Boundary
LOVEL	N5315 W0216	A1 — UA1 — UA251
LUCCO	N5041 W0106	Gatwick Arrivals/Pompi Holds
LUMBA	N5056 E0015	LTMA — Gatwick STARs
LUMEK	N5025 W0031	Y91 — UY90 — UY91
LUSIT	N4913 W0147	Channel Islands CTR
LYNAS	N5326 W0419	Manchester/Liverpool Arrivals
MADLI	N5208 W0258	UN862
MADOX	N5843 W0035	Aberdeen Atlantic Rim

Ident	Co-ordinates	Location
MAGEE	N5447 W0536	Belfast TMA
MALBY	N5135 W0203	B39 — G1
MANGO	N5141 E0047	UR1 — UR12
MANTA	N4942 W0235	Channel Islands CTR
MAPLE	N5223 W0140	Birmingham CTA — Birmingham STARs and SIDs
MARGO	N5442 W0246	B4 — UB4 — UN571 — UN590 — Edinburgh and Glasgow STARs
MASIT	N5420 W1200	North Atlantic Entry Point
MATCH	N5146 E0015	R123 — LTMA — Stansted SIDs
MATIK	N6100 W0804	UN615
MATIM	N5110 W0403	SL3 — SL5
MAYLA	N5137 E0043	LTMA — London City and Biggin Hill STARs
MELEE	N4825 E0222	UG32 (near Paris CDG)
MERLY	N5120 W0500	En route Hold — UA29 — UB40 — UR37 — SL2
MIKEL	N5417 W0452	W928D
MILDE	N5335 W0015	Southern North Sea HMR 9
MIMBI	N5132 W0141	G1 — Farnborough Arrivals (Via CODEY)
MINQI	N4902 W0203	Channel Islands CTR — Jersey Arrivals
MIRSI	N5332 W0243	Manchester/Liverpool Arrivals
MOCHA	N5932 W0121	W5D — Aberdeen ATSU
MOGLI	N5218 W0016	UL613 — UP6
MOLAK	N5436 W0930	UN545 — UN559 — UN569
MONTY	N5253 W0310	A25 — Manchester TMA — Manchester SIDs
MOODY	N5020 W0354	Plymouth Instrument Approach Procedures
MORAY	N5805 W0249	W4D
MORBY	N5355 W0328	W2D
MULIT	N5341 E0328	UL74 — UM604 — UN866
MULLA	N5411 W0544	B2 — Belfast TMA
MYNDA	N5243 W0255	N862 — UN862
NADIR	N5749 0000	P600D
NAKID	N4942 W0437	UG4 — UR116
NANTI	N5308 W0233	B3 — B53 — Manchester TMA — Liverpool SIDs
NASDA	N5034 E0112	A20 — UA20 — London City STARs — Stansted and Luton STARs
NEDUL	N5039 W0133	Solent Control Area Arrivals
NEFYN	N5251 W0044	B39 — UB39
NELSA	N5352 W0211	Leeds/Bradford Departures
NEPTU	N5231 E0250	London/Amsterdam Boundary
NESTA	N6000 W0041	Aberdeen Atlantic Rim
NEVIL	N5000 W0021	G27
NEVIS	N5642 W0433	UN585 — UN601
NIGIT	N5118 W0110	UB39 — UP2
NIPIT	N5427 W0824	UN537
NITON	N5233 W0311	A25 — UA25 — Y98 — UY98
NOBAL	N5715 W0203	Aberdeen ATSU
NOKIN	N5305 W0253	N862 — Y98 — Y99 — UN862 — UY98 — UT99 — Manchester and Liverpool Arrivals
NORBO	N5535 W0445	Glasgow SIDs — Scottish TMA
NORDA	N4947 W0105	Channel Islands CTR
NORLA	N5137 W0651	UR37
NORRY	N5128 W0107	G1 — R41 — UG1 — UR41
NORSE	N6049 E0135	East Shetland Basin Route Structure
NOTRO	N4913 W0646	UT7 — SOTA
NUMPO	N5136 W0316	UA25 — UP2
OLGUD	N5048 W0121	Heathrow/Gatwick Arrivals Bewli Holds
OLIVE	N5224 W0156	Birmingham CTR and CTA — Birmingham STARs
OLKER	N6100 W0630	UN614
OLNEY	N5207 W0043	A20 — B317 — Heathrow SIDs

Ident	Co-ordinates	Location
OMIMI	N4916 W0713	UN512 — SOTA
OMOKO	N4850 W1200	SL1 — SL5 — SOTA
ORIST	N5000 W0150	UR24
ORMER	N4936 W0251	Channel Islands CTR — Guernsey SIDs
ORTAC	N5000 W0200	UR41 — UR84 — UR1 Jersey/Guernsey Arrivals and Departures
ORVIK	N5938 E0039	UG11
OSPOL	N5009 W0011	G27
OYSTA	N4906 W0231	Channel Islands CTR
PAVLO	N5056 W0554	UL3 — UR72
PELIK	N4844 W0410	Brest Control
PEPIS	N5111 W0114	B321 — R41 — UR41
PERCH	N4907 W0157	Channel Islands CTR
PHILI	N4929 W0701	UN502
PIKEY	N4929 W0213	Guernsey Departures
PIKOD	N4925 W0516	UN502
PIRNO	N4948 W0122	B11 Brest Control
PLYMO	N5021 W0438	UR8 En-route Hold
POKIT	N5113 W0001	Luton/Stansted Arrivals
POMPI	N5046 W0057	H51 — UL3 Gatwick Arrivals
POTON	N5205 W0025	B4 — B317 — UB4 — UB317
RADNO	N5214 W0313	A25 — B39 — UA25 — UB39
RANAR	N5340 W0719	Shannon UIR
RANOK	N5642 W0414	W3D
RAPIX	N5126 E0020	UG39
RATKA	N4930 W0800	UN512 — SOTA
REBKA	N4912 W0300	Channel Islands CTR
REDFA	N5206 E0229	R12 — UR12
REGHI	N4800 W0800	Brest Oceanic Transition
REMSI	N5358 W0350	UP6 — UR4
REPLO	N5133 E0108	UA37 — UG39
REXAM	N5304 W0309	A25 — Manchester TMA
RIBEL	N5400 W0217	B4 — Northern Radar Area
RIDLY	N5138 E0005	London City Arrivals
RILKA	N4925 W0620	SL1 — SL4 — SL7

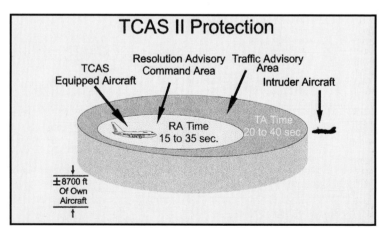

TCAS II Protection

TCAS Equipped Aircraft

Resolution Advisory Command Area

Traffic Advisory Area

Intruder Aircraft

RA Time 15 to 35 sec.

TA Time 20 to 40 sec

±8700 ft Of Own Aircraft

Ident	Co-ordinates	Location
RINGA	N5423 W0534	B2 — B3 — Belfast TMA
RIVAK	N4600 W0800	Brest Oceanic Transition
ROBBO	N5553 W0454	Glasgow SIDs — Scottish TMA
ROBIN	N5257 W0117	B4 — R3 — UB4 — UR3
ROLLS	N5414 E0318	UW538 — UW550
RONAR	N5731 W0539	A1D
RONVI	N5916 W0043	UN584 — UN593 — Hebrides
ROSUN/DALEY	N5340 W0221	Manchester/Liverpool Arrivals
ROWAN	N5145 E0015	LTMA — Stansted SIDs
ROYCE	N5352 E0246	UW534 — UW550
RUPAS	N4930 W0200	Channel Islands CTR — Guernsey SIDs
SABER	N5142 E0057	Heathrow/Stansted/Luton Arrivals
SALCO	N4944 W0331	UA29 — UN863 — UN865
SAMON	N5403 E0347	UA37 — UL7
SANDY	N5103 E0104	A2 — R803 — Heathrow, Stansted and Luton STARs
SAPCO	N5232 W0121	A2 — B53 — East Midlands CTA
SAPOT	N5915 W0222	W3D
SASKI	N5132 E0230	UB29 Amsterdam UIR
SEPAL	N4700 W0845	Brest Oceanic Transition
SETEL	N5400 W0226	A2 — UA2 — Manchester CTR — Manchester and Liverpool STARs
SHAPP	N5430 W0237	B4 — UB4
SHARK	N4911 W0225	Channel Islands CTR — Jersey Arrivals
SHRUB	N5718 W0149	Aberdeen Air Traffic Service
SIDER	N6100 W0508	UG11
SILOK	N5946 W0129	Sumburgh Heli Routes
SILVA	N5358 E0041	UB5 — UR4
SINGA	N5438 E0240	UW538
SIRGO	N5137 E0038	B29 — UB29 — UR12
SITET	N5006 0000	A34 — A56 — R25 — UA34 — UR25
SITKO	N5302 E0253	B1 — UA37 — UB1
SIVIR	N4600 W0845	Brest Oceanic Transition
SKATE	N5500 W0240	UL7 — UL74 — UN591
SKERY	N5000 W0310	A25 — Channel Islands CTR
SKESO	N4949 W0302	UA25 — UN862
SLANY	N5209 W0550	G1 — UG1
SLYDA	N5412 W0505	B3
SMOKI	N5746 W0235	Aberdeen Atlantic Rim — W4D
SODKI	N5847 W0034	Aberdeen Atlantic Rim
SONDO	N5205 E0015	Y6 — UY6
SOTOL	N5502 E0400	UR4
SPEAR	N5134 E0042	LTMA — London City and Biggin Hill STARs
SPIKE	N5732 W0139	Aberdeen ATSU
SPRAT	N5225 E0222	UA37
STAFA	N5251 W0214	B3 — R101 — Birmingham STARs
STIRA	N5608 W0349	Edinburgh/Glasgow Arrivals
STOAT	N5202 W0001	UL613 —UM14
STOCK	N5332 W0149	B1 — Manchester TMA — Manchester/Liverpool SIDs
SUDBY	N5200 E0039	London Terminal Area
SUPAP	N4926 W0549	UN502 — UR72
SWANY	N5133 W0407	UB40 — UR14
TABIT	N5548 W0520	N553D — W958D
TADEX	N5451 W0814	UN551 — UN560
TAKAS	N4900 W0800	UN490 — UN491 — UN508 — SOTA

Ident	Co-ordinates	Location
TALGA	N5157 W0031	A25
TANET	N5126 E0055	A37 — Gatwick STARs
TARAN	N5050 W0201	Heathrow/Gatwick Arrivals Bewli Holds
TARTN	N5542 W0308	Edinburgh STARs — Scottish TMA
TAWNY	N5138 E0009	LTMA — Heathrow STARs — Stansted/Luton Arrivals
TEBRA	N5129 E0136	UG39
TEDSA	N5203 E0108	R77 — UR77
TELBA	N5239 W0219	UA34 — UA251
TESGO	N5011 W0130	SL4 — SL7
THRED	N5030 W0140	Solent Control Arrivals
TIGER	N5104 E0027	Heathrow/Gatwick Arrivals and Departures
TILBY	N5126 E0021	LTMA — London City and Biggin Hill STARs
TILNI	N5432 W0015	Northern Off-Route Area Manchester/Liverpool Arrivals
TIMBA	N5056 E0015	LTMA — Gatwick Arrivals
TINAC	N5615 E0050	UN581
TINAN	N5040 W0033	A25 — Y91 — UA25 — UY91
TIRIK	N5932 W0112	Aberdeen Air Traffic Service
TIVER	N5049 W0325	UA25 — UL3
TIVLI	N5116 W0729	UG4 — G4D
TOBIX	N5136 E0117	Gatwick Arrivals
TOLKA	N5311 W0530	B39 — UB39
TOMMO	N5118 W0002	Heathrow Alternative Hold
TOMPO	N5043 W0333	Exeter Approaches
TOPPA	N5324 E0333	UL74
TOVRI	N4859 W0731	UN491
TRIPO	N5142 E0104	Heathrow, Stansted, Luton, London City and Biggin Arrivals
TROUT	N5730 W0124	En-route Hold — B2D
TULIP	N5222 E0351	R12 Amsterdam FIR
TULTA	N4935 W0800	Shannon Oceanic Transition
TUNBY	N5110 E0019	LTMA — Gatwick SIDs
TUNEL	N5126 E0014	LTMA — Biggin Hill Missed Approach Procedures
TUNIT	N4922 W0300	Channel Islands CTR — Jersey Arrivals and SIDs
TUTON	N5109 W0306	UN862
TWEED	N5540 W0316	Edinburgh STARs — Scottish TMA
TYSTI	N5922 W0011	Aberdeen Approach
ULLAP	N5754 W0510	W6D — Inverness Arrivals
UNROK	N4927 W0630	UN502 — UT7
UPTON	N5335 W0118	B1
VALOG	N4936 W0105	Jersey/Guernsey Arrivals
VAMLA	N6000 W0040	Aberdeen Atlantic Rim
VANIN	N5359 W0402	Isle of Man Arrivals — W2D
VATON	N5125 W0002	Luton/Stansted Arrivals
VATRY	N5233 W0530	R14 — UR14
VAXEL	N5115 E0020	W70 — W71 (for Brussels)
VEULE	N4951 E0037	A1 France Control
WAFFU	N5035 E0021	A47 — G27 — UA47 — UG27
WATFO	N5140 W0002	Northolt Departures
WEALD	N5119 E0002	Heathrow Arrivals
WELIN	N5214 W0051	A2 — A20 — UA2
WESUL	N5140 E0029	UM14 — UR1
WILLO	N5059 W0011	Gatwick Arrivals
WIZAD	N5106 E0057	R8 — Gatwick Departures
WOBUN	N5201 W0044	B3 — Heathrow Departures
WOTAN	N5137 W0220	G1
XAMAB	N5012 E0002	A1 — UA1
XAMAN	N5147 E0021	R1 — UR1

RADIO NAVIGATIONAL AIDS BY IDENTIFICATION

Navigational aids are covered in the following list. The identification is given first, followed by the name, then the type of facility and, finally, its position.
The ident letters are transmitted in morse on a specific frequency for each beacon. These can be found on navigation charts. The third column indicates the purpose. VOR indicates a Very High Frequency Omni-Directional Range. NDBs are more simple non-directional aids, and locators serve a similar purpose.

Ident	Station	Facility	Position
ABB	Abbeville	VOR	N5008 E0151
AC	Glasgow	Locator	N5548 W0432
ADN	Aberdeen/Dyce	VOR/DME	N5718 W0215
ADR	Belfast/Aldergrove	NDB	N5437 W0617
ALD	Alderney	Locator	N4942 W0211
AMB	Amboise	VOR	N4725 E0104
AQ	Aberdeen	NDB	N5708 W0224
ARE	Monts D'Arrée	VOR	N4820 W0336
ATF	Aberdeen	NDB	N5704 W0206
BAL	Baldonnel/Casement	DVOR	N5318 W0627
BCN	Brecon	VOR	N5144 W0316
BDN	Boscombe Down	TACAN	N5109 W0015
BEL	Belfast	VOR	N5440 W0614
BEN	Benbecula	VOR	N5729 W0722
BEZ	Benbecula	TACAN	N5729 W0072
BHD	Berry Head	VOR	N5024 W0330
BHX	Birmingham	Locator	N5228 W0014
BIA	Bournemouth	Locator	N5047 W0015
BIG	Biggin Hill	VOR	N5120 E0002
BKY	Barkway	VOR	N5160 E0004
BLC	Blackbushe	NDB	N5119 W0005
BMH	Bournemouth	NDB	N5046 W0157
BNE	Boulogne	VOR	N5037 E0154
BNN	Bovingdon	VOR	N5143 W0033
BPK	Brookmans Park	VOR	N5145 W0006
BPL	Blackpool	Locator	N5346 W0302
BRI	Bristol	Locator	N5122 W0243
BRR	Barra	NDB	N5702 W0073
BRY	Bray	VOR	N4824 E0317
BUR	Burnham	NDB	N5131 W0040
BV	Brough	NDB	N5344 W0003
BZ	Brize Norton	Locator	N5145 W0136
BZN	Brize Norton	TACAN	N5145 W0014
CAM	Cambridge	Locator	N5213 E0011
CAN	Caen	VOR	N4910 W0027
CBN	Cumbernauld	NDB	N5559 W0036
CDF	Cardiff	Locator	N5124 W0320
CFD	Cranfield	VOR	N5204 W0036
CFN	Donegal	NDB	N5503 W0082
CGY	Coningsby	TACAN	N5305 W0001
CHT	Chiltern	NDB	N5137 W0031
CHW	Chartres	VOR	N4829 E0059
CIT	Cranfield	Locator	N5208 W0033
CL	Carlisle	Locator	N5456 W0248
CLN	Clacton	VOR	N5151 E0109
CML	Clonmel	NDB	N5227 W0073
COA	Costa	VOR	N5121 E0324
COM	Compton Abbas	NDB	N5058 W0021
CON	Connaught	DVOR	N5354 W0849

Ident	Station	Facility	Position
CPT	Compton	VOR	N5129 W0113
CRK	Cork	DVOR	N5150 W0829
CRN	Galway/Carnmore	NDB	N5318 W0086
CSL	Coltishall	TACAN	N5245 E0021
CT	Coventry	Locator	N5225 W0124
CTM	Cottesmore	TACAN	N5244 W0004
CWL	Cranwell	NDB	N5302 W0003
CWZ	Cranwell	TACAN	N5302 W0003
DCS	Dean Cross	VOR	N5443 W0320
DET	Detling	VOR	N5118 E0036
DIK	Diekirch	VOR	N4952 E0608
DIN	Dinard	VOR	N4835 W0205
DND	Dundee	Locator	N5627 W0307
DO	Dounreay/Thurso	NDB	N5835 W0344
DPE	Dieppe	VOR	N4955 E0110
DTY	Daventry	VOR	N5211 W0107
DUB	Dublin	DVOR	N5330 W0618
DVL	Deauville	VOR	N4918 E0018
DVR	Dover	VOR/DME	N5109 E0121
EAS	Southampton/Eastleigh	Locator	N5057 W0121
EDN	Edinburgh	Locator	N5559 W0317
EGT	Eglinton	Locator	N5503 W0071
EKN	Enniskillen	NDB	N5424 W0074
EME	East Midlands	Locator	N5250 W0112
EMW	East Midlands	Locator	N5250 W0127
ENS	Ennis	NDB	N5254 W0855
EPM	Epsom	NDB	N5119 W0022
EX	Exeter	Locator	N5045 W0318
FFA	Fairford	TACAN	N5141 W0015
FOS	Fairoaks	NDB	N5123 W0003
FOY	Foynes	NDB	N5234 W0911
FY	Finningley	NDB	N5329 W0100
GAM	Gamston	VOR	N5317 W0057
GAR	Dublin	NDB	N5332 W0627
GE	Gatwick	NDB	N5110 W0004
GLG	Glasgow	Locator	N5555 W0420
GM	Birmingham	Locator	N5224 W0141
GO	Fife	NDB	N5611 W0031
GOW	Glasgow	VOR	N5552 W0427
GRB	Guernsey	Locator	N4926 W0238
GST	Gloucestershire	Locator	N5153 W0210
GUR	Guernsey	VOR	N4926 W0236
GWC	Goodwood	VOR	N5051 W0045
GY	Gatwick	NDB	N5108 W0019
HAV	Haverfordwest	NDB	N5150 W0458
HAW	Hawarden	Locator	N5311 W0257
HEN	Henton	NDB	N5146 W0005
HB	Belfast City	Locator	N5437 W0553
HBR	Humberside	Locator	N5339 W0018
HG	Halfpenny Green	NDB	N5231 W0215
HON	Honiley	VOR	N5221 W0140
HRW	Heathrow	Locator	N5129 W0003
INS	Inverness	VOR	N5733 W0402
IOM	Isle of Man	VOR	N5404 W0445

Ident	Station	Facility	Position
JSY	Jersey	VOR	N4913 W0203
JW	Jersey	Locator	N4912 W0213
KER	Kerry/Farranfore	NDB	N5210 W0931
KIM	Humberside	Locator	N5334 W0021
KLY	Killiney	NDB	N5316 W0606
KNK	Connaught	NDB	N5354 W0856
KOK	Koksijde	VOR	N5105 E0239
KS	Kinloss	NDB	N5739 W0335
KW	Kirkwall	Locator	N5857 W0254
KWL	Kirkwall	VOR	N5857 W0253
LA	Lyneham	NDB	N5130 W0200
LAM	Lambourne	VOR	N5139 E0009
LAY	Islay	Locator	N5541 W0615
LBA	Leeds/Bradford	Locator	N5352 W0139
LCY	London City	NDB	N5130 E0000
LE	Leicester	NDB	N5236 W0102
LIC	Lichfield	NDB	N5245 W0143
LKH	Lakenheath	TACAN	N5224 E0003
LND	Land's End	VOR	N5008 W0538
LON	London	VOR	N5129 W0028
LPL	Liverpool	NDB	N5320 W0243
LUK	Leuchars	TACAN	N5622 W0025
LUT	Luton	Locator	N5153 W0015
LUX	Luxembourg	VOR	N4937 E0612
LYD	Lydd	VOR	N5060 E0005
LYE	Lyneham	TACAN	N5130 W0016
LYX	Lydd	Locator	N5058 E0057

Below:
The operations room at the Shanwick Oceanic Control Centre at Prestwick. *Civil Aviation Authority*

Ident	Station	Facility	Position
MAC	Machrihanish	DVOR	N5526 W0539
MAY	Mayfield	VOR	N5101 E0007
MCR	Manchester	Locator	N5318 W0222
MCT	Manchester	VOR	N5321 W0216
MID	Midhurst	VOR	N5103 W0037
MLD	Mildenhall	TACAN	N5222 E0003
MW	Middle Wallop	NDB	N5109 W0133
ND	Great Yarmouth	Locator	N5238 E0143
NEW	Newcastle	VOR	N5502 W0142
NGY	New Galloway	NDB	N5511 W0410
NH	Norwich	Locator	N5241 E0123
NOT	Nottingham	NDB	N5255 W0105
NTM	Nattenheim	VOR	N5000 E0632
OB	Cork	Locator	N5145 W0826
OC	Cork	Locator	N5154 W0832
OCK	Ockham	VOR	N5118 W0027
OF	Filton	Locator	N5131 W0235
OK	Connaught	NDB	N5355 W0842
OL	Shannon	Locator	N5245 W0849
OP	Dublin	Locator	N5325 W0061
OTR	Ottringham	VOR	N5342 W0006
OW	Heathrow	NDB	N5128 W0035
OX	Oxford Kidlington	Locator	N5150 W0119
OY	Belfast Aldergrove	Locator	N5441 W0605
PIK	Prestwick	NDB	N5530 W0043
PLY	Plymouth	Locator	N5025 W0041
POL	Pole Hill	VOR	N5344 W0206
PSW	Ipswich	NDB	N5202 E0112
PTH	Perth/Scone	VOR	N5626 W0322
PW	Prestwick	Locator	N5533 W0441
PY	Plymouth	Locator	N5025 W0407
RDL	Redhill	NDB	N5113 W0001
REM	Reims	VOR	N4918 E0402
RNR	Radnor	NDB	N5214 W0315
ROU	Rouen	VOR	N4928 E0117
RSH	Rush (Dublin)	NDB	N5331 W0607
RWY	Ronaldsway	Locator	N5405 W0436
SAB	St Abbs	VOR	N5554 W0212
SAM	Southampton	VOR	N5057 W0121
SAT	St Athan	TACAN	N5124 W0033
SAY	Stornoway	NDB	N5813 W0619
SBH	Sumburgh	Locator	N5953 W0118
SDM	Shipdam	NDB	N5237 E0006
SFD	Seaford	VOR	N5045 E0007
SHA	Shannon	DVOR	N5243 W0854
SHD	Scotstownhead	NDB	N5734 W0149
SHM	Shoreham	Locator	N5050 W0018
SLG	Sligo	NDB	N5417 W0836
SM	St Mawgan	NDB	N5026 W0459
SND	Southend	NDB	N5134 E0042
SPI	Sprimont	VOR	N5030 E0537
SSD	Stansted	NDB	N5154 E0001
STM	Isles of Scilly	Locator	N4955 W0617
STN	Stornoway	VOR	N5812 W0611
STU	Strumble	VOR	N5160 W0502

Ident	Station	Facility	Position
SUM	Sumburgh	VOR	N5953 W0117
SWB	Shawbury	VOR	N5248 W0024
SWN	Swansea	Locator	N5136 W0404
TD	Teesside	Locator	N5434 W0120
TIR	Tiree	VOR	N5630 W0652
TL	Lerwick/Tingwall	NDB	N6011 W0011
TLA	Talla	VOR	N5530 W0321
TNT	Trent	VOR	N5303 W0140
TRN	Turnberry	VOR	N5519 W0447
UW	Edinburgh	Locator	N5554 W0330
WAL	Wallasey	VOR	N5323 W0308
WCO	Westcott	NDB	N5151 W0058
WFD	Woodford	NDB	N5320 W0209
WFR	West Freugh	Locator	N5452 W0045
WHI	Whitegate	NDB	N5311 W0237
WIK	Wick	VOR	N5827 W0306
WIT	Wittering	TACAN	N5236 W0003
WL	Barrow/Walney Island	NDB	N5408 W0316
WOD	Woodley	NDB	N5127 W0053
WPL	Welshpool	NDB	N5238 W0031
WTD	Waterford	NDB	N5211 W0705
WTM	Wattisham	TACAN	N5207 E0006
WTN	Warton	Locator	N5345 W0251
WZ	Newcastle	Locator	N5500 W0148
YVL	Yeovil	Locator	N5056 W0240

Below:
The operations room for the Shanwick Oceanic Control at Prestwick. *Civil Aviation Authority*

Appendix VI: Airline Callsigns

This appendix lists most of the airlines which operate in UK airspace. In most cases the callsign will incorporate the name of the operator but there are quite a number of exceptions, the best known being British Airways which uses the callsigns 'Speedbird' or 'Shuttle'. Flights are normally identified by a two-, three- or four-character number after the callsign name and usually this number relates to the airline timetable. However, there is a growing tendency for some airlines to use numbers which have no relationship to their timetable, therefore the airband listener will find it difficult to identify some flights. Publications are available which are invaluable in providing a decode for flight numbers and some of these listings include UK overflights.

The callsigns listed are current at the time of publication, but unfortunately they are subject to change. (I am indebted to Aviation Data Research and Javiation of Bradford for their assistance in keeping the list up to date).

Callsign	Airline	Callsign	Airline
Abbas	Abbas Air	Alidair	Alidair
Abex	Airborne Express	Alitalia	Alitalia
Adria	Adria Airways	American	American
Advent	ATS/Vulcan	Amiri	Qatar Government/
Aerocharter	Aero Charter Midlands		Royal Flight
	Limited	AmTran	American Tans Air
Aero Croat	Aero Croatia	Army Air	Army Air Corps
Aeroflot	Aeroflot	Ascot	Royal Air Force Transport
Aeronaut	Cranfield Institute of	Asia	Japan Asia Airlines
	Technology	Aspro	Intereuropean Airways
Air Algeria	Air Algeria	Atlantic	Air Atlantique
Air Atlantique	Air Atlantique	Austrian	Austrian
Air Bahama	Air Bahama	Aviaco	Aviaco
Air Berlin	Air Berlin	Avro	British Aerospace
Air Bridge	Hunting Cargo		Woodford
Air Canada	Air Canada	Ayline	Aurigny Air Services
Air Chester	City Air	Aztec Air	Air Bristol
Aircom	Air Commuter	Backer	British Charter
Air Discovery	Discovery Airways	Bafair	Belgian Air Force
Air Ecosse	Air Ecosse	Bafjet	British Air Ferries
Air España	Air España		Business Jets
Air Europe	Air Europe	Bahrain One	The Amiri Royal Flight
Air Express	Air Express	Balair	Balair
Air Ferry	British World Airlines	Balkan	Balkan
Air Force 1	USAF (President)	Bangladesh	Bangladesh
Air Force 2	USAF (Vice-President)	Bea Tours	Caledonian Airways
Air France	Air France	Beech Air	Beecham Group
Air India	Air India	Beeline	Biggin Hill Executive
Air Jamaica	Air Jamaica		Aviation
Air Lanka	Air Lanka	Bee-Wee	British West Indian Airways
Airlift	Airlift	Belgian Air Force	Belgian Air Force
Air London	Air London	Beryl	Emerald Air
Air Malta	Air Malta	Big A	Arrow Air
Air Maroc	Royal Air Maroc	Biggles	Express Air Charter
Air Mauritius	Air Mauritius	Blue Eagle	Eagle Air
Air Mexico	Aeromexico	Bristow	Bristow Helicopter Group
Air Mike	Continental Micronesia	Britannia	Britannia
Air New Zealand	Air New Zealand	British Island	British Island Airways
Air Portugal	Air Portugal (TAP)	Caledonian	Caledonian Airways Ltd.
Airtax	Birmingham Aviation	Calibrator	CAA Calibration Flight
Airwork	Airwork Services Training	Caljet	Calair
Air Zaire	Air Zaire	Camair	Cameroon Airlines
		Canadian	Canadian Airlines

Call Sign	Airline	Call Sign	Airline
Canadian Military	Canadian Military	Hapag Lloyd	Hapag Lloyd
Capital	Capital	Hawaiian	Hawaiian
Cargolux	Cargolux	Heavy Lift	Heavy Lift
Crribbean	Carribbean	Hotair	Baltic Airlines
Cathay	Cathay Pacific	Iberia	Iberia
Celtic	Celtic Airways	Iceair	Icelandair
Centreline	Centreline Air Services	Indonesia	Garuda
Channel	Channel	Intercity	Intercity
Channex	Channel Express	Iranair	Iranair
China	China Airlines	Iraqi	Iraqi
CIL	Cecil Aviation	Irish Air Corps	Irish Air Corps
City	KLM Cityhopper	Israeli Air Force	Israeli Air Force
City Ireland	Cityjet	Italian Air Force	Italian Air Force
City Flite	City Airways	Itavia	Itavia
Clansman	Airwork	Jan	Janus Airways
Clanspeed	Scottish European Airways	Japanair	Japan Airlines
Clifton	Bristol Flying Centre	Jersey	Jersey European
Colours	Flying Colours	Jetset	Air 2000
Compass	Compass Aviation	Jetstar	Jetstar
Compass	Compass Helicopters, Bristol	Jordanian	Alia Royal Jordanian
Condor	C ondor	Juliett Juliett	Avio Genex
Continental	Continental	Juliett Papa	Inex Adria Avio Promet
Crossair	Crossair	Kenya	Kenya
CSA/		Kestrel	Airtours International
Czechoslovakian	CSA	Kilro	Air Kilroe
Cubana	Cubanair	Kite	Kite
Cyprus	Cyprus	Kitty/Kittyhawk	Queen's Flight
Delta	Delta	Kiwi	Royal New Zealand Air Force
Directflight	Directflight		
Dynasty	China Air Lines	KLM	KLM
Eagle	Eagle Flying Services	Korean	Korean
Eastern	Eastern	Kuwait	Kuwait
Easy	Easyjet	Libyan	Libyan
Echo Jet	Berlin European	Logan	Loganair
Egyptair	Egyptair	Lot	Lot
El Al	El Al	Lufthansa	Lufthansa
Ethiopian	Ethiopian	Luxair	Luxair
Euroair	Euroair	Lyddair	World Executive Airways
Euroflite	Euroflite	Maersk	Maersk Air
Euromanx	Manx Airlines (Europe)	MAC	Military Airlift Command v USA
Europa	Air Europa		
European	London European	Macline	McAlpine Limited
Evergreen	Evergreen	Malaysian	Malaysian
Evergreen	Evergreen International Airlines	Malev	Malev
		Manx	Manx Airlines
Exam	CAA Flight Examiners	Martinair	Martinair
Express	Federal Express	Medivac	London Helicopter Emergency Service
Expressair	Expressair Services		
Fairflight	Fairflight	Merlin	Rolls-Royce
Fanum	Automobile Association	Merrix	Eagle European Airways/Merrix Air Ltd
Federal Express	Federal Express		
Finnair	Finnair	Metropolitan	Metropolitan
Fordair	Ford Motor Company	Middle East	Middle East
Genair	Genair	Midland	British Midland
German Air Force	German Air Force	Minair	CAA Flying Unit
Ghana	Ghana	Monarch	Monarch
Gibair	GB Airways	Montana	Montana
Global	Global	Nationair	Nation Air
Granite	Business Air	National	National Airways
Guernsey	Guernsey Airlines	Navy	Royal Navy
Gulf Air	Gulf Air		
Gulf Stream	Gulf Stream		

Call Sign	Airline	Call Sign	Airline
Nigerian	Nigerian	Speedwing	Deutsche BA
Nitro	TNT	Springbok	South African Airways
Northwest	Northwest	Starjet	Novair International
Ocean	Atlantic Aviation	Stol	London City Airways
Olympia	Olympia	Sudan	Sudan Airways
Orange	Air Holland	Swissair	Swissair
Orion	Orion	Syrian	Syrian Air
Pacific Western	Pacific Western	Tarom	Tarom
Pakistan	Pakistan	Teastar	TEA
Parachute	UK Parachute Centre	Tester	Empire Test Pilots School, Boscombe Down
Paramount	Paramount		
Piedmont	Piedmont	Thai	Thai
Qantas	Qantas	Tradewinds	Tradewinds
Quebecair	Quebecair	Transamerica	Transamerica
Rafair	Royal Air Force	Tunis	Tunis
Rainbow	Royal Air Force (Duke of Edinburgh)	TWA	Trans World Airlines
		Uganda	Uganda
Romanian	Romanian	Ukay	Air UK
Rosie	Rosenbalm/Emery	UK Leisure	Air UK Leisure
Ryanair	Ryanair	United	United
Sabena	Sabena	UPS	United Parcel Service
Sam	Sam	UTA	UTA
Sapphire	British Aerospace (Filton)	Varig	Varig
Saudi	Saudi	Vernair	Vernons Pools
Scandinavian	Scandinavian	Viasa	Viasa
Scotair	Air Charter (Scotland)	Vickers	Vickers
Scottish Express	Scottish Express	Viking	Scanair
Shamrock	Air Lingus	Virgin	Virgin
Short	Short Brothers	Viva	Viva Air
Shuttle 2	BA Shuttle LHR-Manchester	Watchdog	Ministry of Agriculture, Fisheries & Food
Shuttle 3	BA Shuttle Manchester-LHR		
		Western	Western
Shuttle 4	BA Shuttle LHR-Belfast	West Indian	West Indian
Shuttle 5	BA Shuttle Belfast-LHR	World	World
Shuttle 6	BA Shuttle LHR-Glasgow	Worldways	Worldways
Shuttle 7	BA Shuttle Glasgow-LHR	Yemen	Yemen
Shuttle 8	BA Shuttle LHR-Edinburgh	Yugair	Air Yugoslavia/JAT
Shuttle 9	BA Shuttle Edinburgh-LHR	Zaire	Zaire
Sierra Leone	Sierra Leone	Zambia	Zambia
Singapore	Singapore Airlines	Zimbabwe	Air Zimbabwe
Skyship	Airship Industries		
Spacegrand	Spacegrand Aviation		
Special Support	Metropolitan Police Air		
Speedbird	British Airways		

Below:
Japan Airlines 747. *Japan Airlines*

Appendix VII: Voice Weather Broadcasts

A — Actual weather report
S — Sigmet

F — Landing forecast
T — Forecast trend type

Location	Broadcast time	Info	Airports covered
CROUGHTON 6750 H24 11176 H24 13214 08-2100	H+25 & +55	T	Lajes, Mildenhall, Ramstein, Rhein Main
DUBLIN 127.0 H24	Continuous	AFT	Dublin, Shannon, Cork, Belfast, Glasgow, Prestwick, Manchester, London/Heathrow, LondonGatwick
GANDER 3485 H24 6604 H24	H+20/25	F A	Montreal/Mirabel, Toronto, Ottawa Montreal/Mirabel, Toronto, Gander, Ottawa, Goose
10051 H24 13270 H24	H+25/30	A	Winnipeg, Edmonton, Calgary, Churchill Kuujjuaq, Winnipeg, Churchill
	H+50/55	F A	Gander, St Johns, Halifax Montreal/Mirabel, Gander, Stephenville, Halifax, St Johns
	H+55/60	FS A	Goose, Iqaluit, Sondrestrom Goose, Iqaluit, Sondrestrom, Kuujjuaq
LAJES 6750 H24 8967 H24 13244 10-2100	H+00 & +30	T	Lajes, Mildenhall, Ramstein, Rhein Main
LONDON (MAIN) 135.375 H24	Continuous	AT	Amsterdam, Brussels, Dublin, Glasgow, London/Gatwick, London/Heathrow, London/Stansted, Manchester, Paris/Charles de Gaulle
LONDON (SOUTH) 128.6 H24	Continuous	AT	Birmingham, Bournemouth, Bristol, Cardiff, Jersey, Luton, Norwich, Southampton, Southend
LONDON (NORTH) 126.6 H24	Continuous	AT	Blackpool, East Midlands, Leeds/Bradford, Liverpool, London/Gatwick, Manchester, Newcastle, Isle of Man/Ronaldsway, Teesside
NEW YORK 3485 H24 6604 H24 13270 H24	H+00	F A	Detroit, Chicago, Cleveland Detroit, Chicago, Cleveland, Niagara Falls, Milwaukee, Indianapolis

Location	Broadcast time	Info	Airports covered
10051 H24			
	H+05	FS	Bangor, Pittsburgh, Charlotte
		AS	Bangor, Pittsburgh, Windsor Locks, St Louis, Charlotte, Minneapolis
	H+10	F	New York, Newark, Boston
		A	New York, Newark, Boston, Baltimore, Philadelphia, Washington
	H+15	FS	Bermuda Nas, Miami, Atlanta
		AS	Bermuda Nas, Miami, Nassau, Freeport, Tampa, West Palm Beach, Atlanta
	H+30	F	Niagara Falls, Milwaukee, Indianapolis
		A	Detroit, Chicago, Cleveland, Niagara Falls, Milwaukee, Indianapolis
	H+35	FS	Windsor Locks, St Louis
		AS	Bangor, Pittsburgh, Windsor Locks, St Louis, Charlotte, Minneapolis
	H+40	F	Baltimore, Philadelphia, Washington
		A	New York, Newark, Boston, Baltimore, Philadelphia, Washington
	H+45	FS	Nassau, Freeport
		AS	Bermuda Nas, Miami, Nassau, Freeport, Tampa, West Palm Beach, Atlanta
SCOTTISH 125.725 H24	Continuous	AT	Aberdeen, Belfast/Aldergrove, Edinburgh, Glasgow, Inverness, London/Heathrow, Prestwick, Stornoway, Sumburgh
SHANNON 3413 HN 5505 H24 8957 H24 13264 HJ	H+00	FS	Brussels Ntl, Hamburg
		AS	Brussels Ntl, Hamburg Frankfurt (Main), Cologne Bonn, Düsseldorf, Munich
	H+05	F	Shannon, Prestwick, London/Heathrow
		A	Shannon, Prestwick, London/Heathrow, Amsterdam/Schiphol, Manchester, London/Gatwick
	H+10	AS	Copenhagen/Kastrup, Stockholm/Arlanda, Gothenburg/Landvetter, Bergen/Flesland, Oslo/Gardemoen, Helsinki/Vantaa, Dublin, Barcelona
	H+15	F	Madrid/Barajas, Lisbon, Paris/Orly
		A	Madrid/Barajas, Lisbon, Santa Maria, Paris/Orly, Paris/Charles de Gaulle, Lyon/Satolas
	H+20/25	FS	Rome/Fiumicino, Milan/Malpensa
		AS	Rome/Fiumicino, Milan/Malpensa, Zurich, Geneva/Cointrin, Turin/Caselle, Keflavik

Location	Broadcast time	Info	Airports covered
	H+30	FS	Frankfurt (Main), Cologne/Bonn
		AS	Brussels Ntl, Hamburg, Frankfurt (Main), Cologne/Bonn, Düsseldorf, Munich
	H+35	F	Amsterdam/Schiphol, Manchester, London/Gatwick
		A	Shannon, Prestwick, London/Heathrow, Amsterdam/Schiphol, Manchester, London/Gatwick
	H+40	AS	Copenhagen/Kastrup, Stockholm/Arlanda, Gothenburg/Landvetter, Bergen/Flesland, Oslo/Gardemoen, Helsinki/Vantaa, Dublin, Barcelona
	H+45	F	Santa Maria, Athens, Paris/Charles de Gaulle
		A	Madrid/Barajas, Lisbon, Santa Maria, Paris/Orly, Paris/Charles de Gaulle, Lyon/Satolas
	H+50/55	FS	Zurich, Geneva/Cointrin
		AS	Rome/Fiumicino, Milan/Malpensa, Zurich, Geneva/Cointrin, Turin/Caselle, Keflavik

TRENTON (MILITARY)

15034 1000-0000 6754 2300-1100	H+30	AT*	Gander/Halifax/Shearwater Greenwood/Bagotville/Trenton/Ottawa/ Toronto/Winnipeg/Edmonton/Cold Lake, Comox/Victoria/Abbotsford

* T — if time permits

ROYAL AIR FORCE

5450 H24 11253 H24	Continuous Continuous	A	Belfast/Aldergrove, Benson Brize Norton, Finningley, Kinloss, Leuchars, London/Heathrow, Lyneham, Manchester, Northolt, Odiham, Prestwick, St Mawgan, Waddington, Wyton, Düsseldorf, Laarbruch, Keflavik, Ascension

Note:
1. H24 indicates that the broadcast is continuous.
2. H+ minutes indicates the time at which the broadcast commences, eg H+25 means that the broadcast takes place at 25min past each hour.

Appendix VIII: Worldwide High Frequency Coverage

The following listings cover HF aeronautical channels for different regions of the world. Each region is followed by the radio stations within the network and the various allocated frequencies. Note, however, that the full range of frequencies will not normally be covered by every station within the group.

North Atlantic 'A'
NAT-A
CANARIES, GANDER, NEW YORK, PARAMARIBO, PIARCO, SANTA MARIA, SHANWICK
2962, 3016, 5598, 6533, 6628, 8825, 8906, 13306, 17946

North Atlantic 'B'
NAT-B
GANDER, REYKJAVIK, SHANWICK
2899, 5616, 8864, 13291, 17946

North Atlantic 'C'
NAT-C
GANDER, REYKJAVIK, SHANWICK
2872, 5649, 8879, 11336, 13306, 17946

North Atlantic 'D'
NAT-D
BODO, BAFFIN, CHURCHILL, IQALUIT, KANGERLUSSUAQ, REYKJAVIK, SHANWICK
2971, 2983, 4666, 4675, 6544, 8840, 8891, 11279, 13291, 17946

North Atlantic 'E'
NAT-E
NEW YORK, SANTA MARIA
2962, 6628, 8825, 11309, 13354, 17946

North Atlantic 'F'
NAT-F
GANDER, SHANWICK
3476, 6622, 8831, 13291, 17946

Europe
EUR
MALTA, TUNIS
5661, 10084

Middle East 1
MID-1
ADEN, AMMAN, BAGHDAD, BAHRAIN, BASRAH, JEDDAH, KUWAIT, RIYAN, SANAA, TEHRAN
2992, 3404, 5603, 5667, 8847, 8918, 13312, 13336

Middle East 2
MID-2
BAHRAIN, DELHI, ISLAMABAD, KABUL, KARACHI, KATHMANDU, KUWAIT, LAHORE, MALE, MUMBAI, MUSCAT, PESHAWAR, SEYCHELLES, SHIRAZ, TEHRAN
2923, 3467, 5601, 5658, 7595, 10018, 13288

African 1
AFI-1
ABIDJAN, BAMAKO, BISSAU, BOBO, CANARIES, CASABLANCA, CONAKRY, DAKAR, FREETOWN, KORHOGO, MONROVIA/ROBERTS, NOUADHIBOU, NOUAKCHOTT, OUAGADOUGOU, SAL
3452, 6535, 6573, 6589, 8861, 13357, 17955

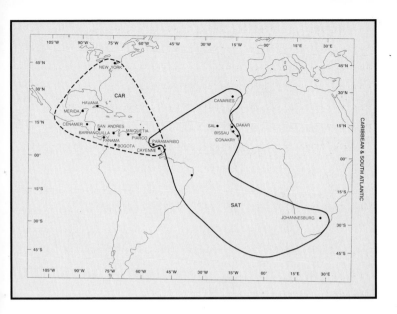

Above:
High frequency radio coverage — the Caribbean.
Royal Air Force

Below:
High frequency radio coverage — South America.
Royal Air Force

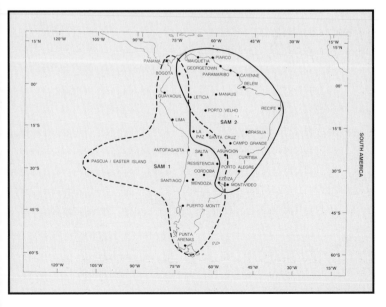

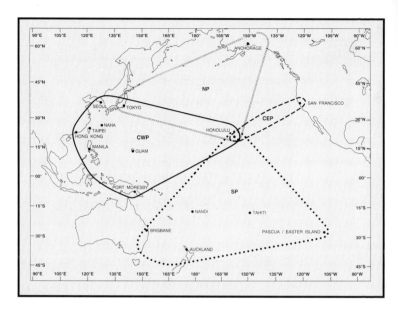

Above:
High frequency radio coverage — the Pacific.
Royal Air Force

Below:
High frequency radio coverage — Africa (1, 2, 4).
Royal Air Force

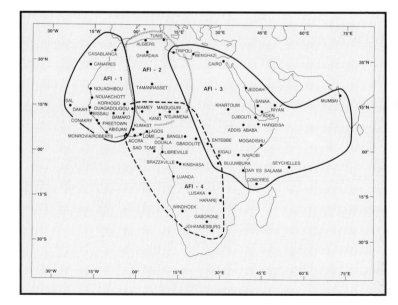

African 2

AFI-2

ALGIERS, GAO, GHARDAIA, KANO, MAIDUGURI, N'DJAMENA, NIAMEY, TAMANRASSET, TRIPOLI, TUNIS

3419, 5652, 5680, 8873, 8894, 13273, 17961

African 3

AFI-3

ADDIS ABABA, ADEN, ASMARA, BENGHAZI, BUJUMBURA, CAIRO, COMORES, DAR ES SALAAM, DJIBOUTI, ENTEBBE, HARGEISA, JEDDAH, KHARTOUM, KIGALI, MOGADISHU, MUMBAI, NAIROBI, RIYAN, SANA'A, SEYCHELLES, TRIPOLI

3467, 5505, 5517, 5540, 5658, 6574, 7595, 8854, 8870, 8959, 10025, 11300, 13288, 17961

African 4

AFI-4

ABIDJAN, ACCRA, BANGUI, BATA, BRAZZAVILLE, BUJUMBURA, DOUALA, ENTEBBE, GABORONE, GBADOLITE, HARARE, JOHANNESBURG, KANO, KINSHASA, KUMASI, LAGOS, LIBREVILLE, LILONGWE, LOME, LUANDA, LUSAKA, MAIDUGURI, MALABO, NAIROBI, N'DJAMENA, NIAMEY, OUAGADOUGOU, SAO TOME, TAKORADI, TAMALE, WINDHOEK

2851, 2878, 5493, 6559, 6586, 6879, 8861, 8873, 8888, 8903, 9495, 13294

African 5/Indian Ocean 1

AFI-5/INO-1

ANTANANARIVO, BUJUMBURA, COCOS, COLOMBO, COMORES, DAR ES SALAAM, HARARE, JOHANNESBURG, LUSAKA, MAHAJANGA, MAURITIUS, MUMBAI, NAIROBI, PERTH, ST DENIS, SEYCHELLES, TOAMASINA

2376, 3425, 3476, 3682, 4657, 5634, 6915, 7595, 8849, 8861, 8879, 10018, 11300, 13306, 17961, 21926

South East Asia 1

SEA-1

CALCUTTA, COCOS, COLOMBO, DHAKA, JAKARTA, KATHMANDU, KUALA LUMPUR, MADRAS, MALE, SINGAPORE, TRIVANDRUM, YANGON

2947, 3470, 3491, 5670, 6556, 10066, 11285, 13318, 17907

South East Asia 2

SEA-2

BANGKOK, HO CHI MINH, HONG KONG, KINABALU, KUALA LUMPUR, MANILA, SINGAPORE, VIENTIANE

3485, 5655, 8942, 11396, 13309

South Asia 3

SEA-3

BALI, CALCUTTA, COCOS, DARWIN, JAKARTA, MALE, PERTH, SINGAPORE, TRIVANDRUM, UJUNG PANDANG

3470, 6556, 11285, 11396, 13318, 17907

Central West Pacific

CWP

GUAM, HONG KONG, HONOLULU, MANILA, NAHA, PORT MORESBY, SEOUL, TAIPEI, TOKYO

2998, 3455, 4666, 6532, 8903, 11384, 13300, 17904

North Pacific

NP

ANCHORAGE, HONOLULU, TOKYO

2932, 5628, 6655, 8915, 8951, 10048, 11330, 13273, 13294, 21925

Central Pacific

CEP

HONOLULU, SAN FRANCISCO

2869, 3413, 5547, 5574, 6673, 8843, 10057, 11282, 13288, 13354, 17904

South Pacific
SP
AUCKLAND, HONOLULU, NANDI, PASCUA/EASTER ISLAND, BRISBANE, TAHITI
3467, 5643, 8867, 13261, 13300, 17904

South America 1
SAM-1
ANTOFAGASTA, ASUNCION, BOGOTA, CORDOBA, EZEIZA/BUENOS AIRES, GUAYAQUIL, LA PAZ, LIMA, MENDOZA, PANAMA, PASCUA/EASTER ISLAND, PUERTO MONTT, PUNTA ARENAS, RESISTENCIA, SALTA, SANTA CRUZ, SANTIAGO
2944, 4669, 5454, 5583, 5595, 5604, 6649, 6535, 10024, 10066, 11360, 17907

South America 2
SAM-2
ASUNCION, BELEM, BOGOTA, BRASILIA, CAMPO GRANDE, CAYENNE, CURITIBA, EZEIZA/BUENOS AIRES, GEORGE TOWN, LA PAZ, LETICIA, MAIQUETIA, MANAUS, MONTEVIDEO, PARAMARIBO, PIARCO, PORTO ALEGRE, PORTO VELHO, RECIFE, SANTA CRUZ
3479, 3488, 5526, 6533, 8855, 8894, 10096, 13297, 17907

Caribbean
CAR
BARRANQUILLA, BOGOTA, CAYENNE, CENAMER, HAVANA, MAIQUETIA, MERIDA, NEW YORK, PANAMA, PARAMARIBO, PIARCO, SAN ANDRES
2887, 5520, 5550, 6532, 6577, 6728, 8918, 10017, 11387, 11396, 13297, 13339, 17907

South Atlantic
SAT
ABIDJAN, BISSAU, CANARIES, CONAKRY, DAKAR, JOHANNESBURG, PARAMARIBO, RECIFE, SAL, SAO TOME
2854, 3432, 3452, 5565, 6535, 8861, 11291, 13315, 13357, 17955, 21926

Miscellaneous HF Frequencies

RAF FLIGHT WATCH CENTRES
RAF KINLOSS AND RAF BAMPTON CASTLE (CALLSIGN 'ARCHITECT')
2591, 4540, 4742, 5714, 6739, 8190, 9031, 11205, 11247, 13257, 15031, 18018

ASCENSION (CALLSIGN 'HAVEN')
4742, 9031, 11247

CYPRUS (CALLSIGN 'CYPRUS')
4742, 9031, 11247

GIBRALTAR (CALLSIGN 'GIBRALTAR')
4742, 11247

MOUNT PLEASANT (FALKLANDS) (CALLSIGN 'VIPER')
9031, 11247

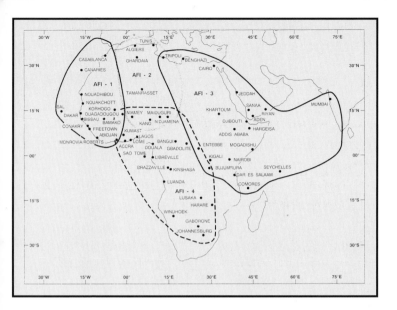

Above:
High frequency radio coverage — Africa (1, 3).
Royal Air Force

Below:
High frequency radio coverage — Europe/Middle
East. *Royal Air Force*

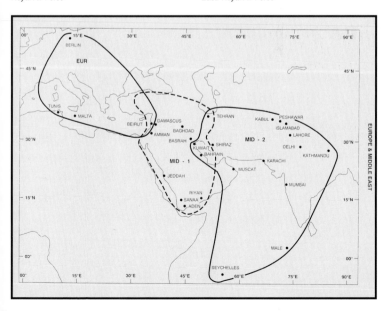

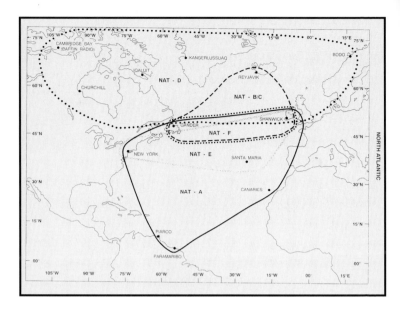

Above:
High frequency radio coverage — North Atlantic.
Royal Air Force

Below:
High frequency radio coverage — Indian Ocean.
Royal Air Force

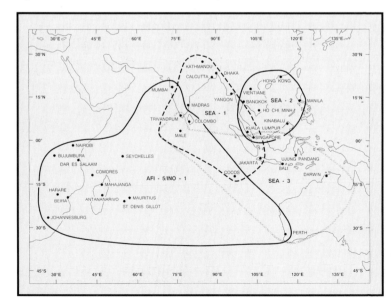

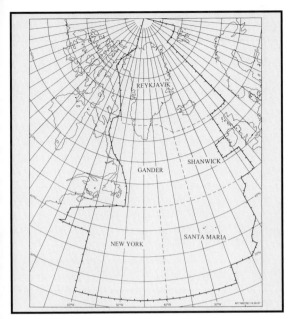

Left:
The North Atlantic
areas of responsibility.
Civil Aviation Authority

Below:
An example of a day-
time westbound tracks
over the North Atlantic.
Civil Aviation Authority

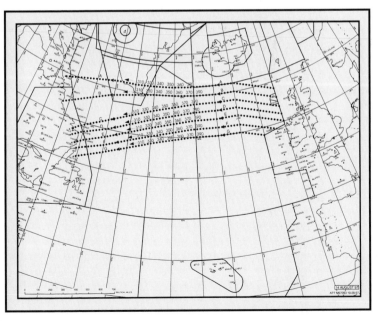

Appendix IX: Company Frequencies

All flights need to speak to their operational base from time to time on matters not related to air traffic control.

Specific frequencies are set aside for this purpose, both on VHF and HF. Those on VHF are almost all between 130MHz and 132MHz, with a small number in the 136MHz range, while those on HF are spread throughout the band.

Many companies who do not have their own radio-equipped bases are able to keep in contact by using message-handling agencies (eg Servisair), sometimes being connected to their bases by land-line.

On HF there are many kinds of messages being transmitted on the company frequencies, often via handling agencies such as Stockholm Radio and Berne Radio.

VHF Company Frequencies

Handling Organisations

130.600	Servisair	131.600	TWA (LGW)
130.650	Gatwick Handling (several airlines)	131.625	Speedbird South (LGW)
		131.650	Japan Air (LHR)
130.650	Manchester Handling		KLM (LHR)
131.625	Portishead	131.675	Britannia (LGW)
		131.700	Scandinavian (LHR)
Airlines			Swissair (LHR)
131.425	Air New Zealand (LHR)	131.750	Shamrock (Aer Lingus) (LHR)
	British Midland (LHR)		Air UK (LHR)
	Virgin (LHR)		Continental (LHR)
	Servisair (Birmingham)	131.800	Speedbird (LHR)
131.450	Air Canada (LHR)	131.825	Stansted Handling
	Alitalia (LHR)	131.850	Speedbird (Manchester)
	Pakistan (LHR)		Singapore (LHR)
131.475	Sabena (LHR)	131.875	Qantas (LHR)
	Speedbird North (LGW)	131.900	Speedbird Long Haul (LHR)
131.500	Air France (LHR)	131.925	Air India (LHR)
	Aer Lingus		Lufthansa (LHR)
	Aeroflot	131.950	Iberia (LHR)
	Air Portugal	131.975	Air Jamaica (LHR)
131.525	American (LHR)		United (LHR)
131.550	Speedbird (LHR)	136.850	Britannia
		136.875	Monarch

HF Company Frequencies

Berne (Switzerland)	4654, 6643, 8936, 10069, 13205, 15046, 18023, 21988, 23285
Stockholm (Sweden)	3494, 5541, 8930, 11345, 13342, 17916, 23210
British Airways (London)	5535, 8921, 10072, 13333, 17922, 21948
Rainbow (Canada)	3458, 5604, 8819, 10264, 13285, 13339, 13420, 17910

Note: Many more frequencies are obtainable from specialist books, available from several of the companies listed at the end of the book. Amateur radio magazines also carry advertisements for frequency publications.

Opposite Top:
Manchester ATCC. *Civil Aviation Authority*

Opposite Bottom:
Low level airways structure over London and Birmingham. *Royal Air Force*

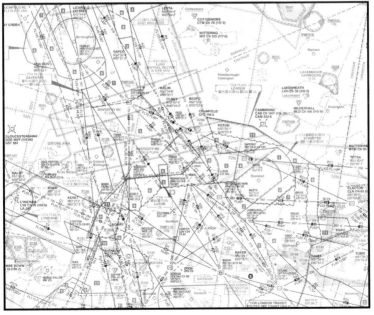

Appendix X: Useful Addresses

Most of the following companies supply receivers and other equipment related to airband listening. Contact them for comprehensive catalogues and price lists. Many of the suppliers can also offer secondhand items.

Air Supply,
97 High Street,
YEADON,
Leeds LS19 7TA
Tel: (0113) 250 9581

Amateur Radio Communications Limited,
38 Bridge Street,
EARLESTOWN,
Newton-le-Willows,
Merseyside WA12 9BA
Tel: (01925) 229881
Fax: (01925) 229882

AOR UK Limited,
4E East Mill,
Bridgefoot,
BELPER,
Derbyshire DE56 2UA
Tel: (01773) 880788
Fax: (01773) 880780

ARE Communications,
6 Royal Parade,
Hanger Lane,
EALING,
LONDON W5A 1ET
Tel: (0181) 997 4476

ASK Electronics Limited,
248 Tottenham Court Road,
LONDON W1P 9AD
Tel: (0171) 637 0353
Fax: (0171) 637 2690

The Aviation Hobby Centre,
Visitors Centre,
Main Terminal,
Birmingham International Airport,
BIRMINGHAM B26 3QJ
Tel: (0121) 782 2112
Fax: (0121) 782 6423

The Aviation Hobby Shop,
4 Horton Parade,
Horton Road,
West Drayton,
Middlesex UB7 8EA
Tel: (01895) 442123

Communication Centre,
(Photo Acoustics Limited),
58 High Street,
NEWPORT PAGNELL,
Bucks MK16 8AQ
Tel: (01908) 610625
Fax: (01908) 216373

Flightdeck,
The Airband Shop,
252A Finney Lane,
Heald Green,
CHEADLE,
Cheshire SK8 3QD
Tel: (0161) 499 9350
Fax: (0161) 499 9349

Right:
The new Swanwick Air Traffic Control Centre.
Civil Aviation Authority

Below:
Landing chart for Yeovilton RNAS. *Aerad*

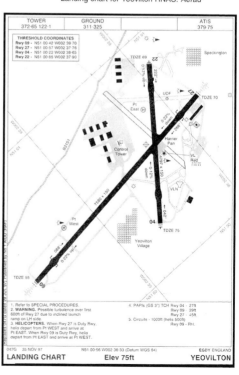

Garex Electronics,
Unit 8,
Sandpiper Court,
Harrington Lane,
EXETER EX4 8NS
Tel: (01392) 466899
Fax: (01392) 466887

Haydon Communications,
132 High Street,
EDGWARE,
Middlesex HA8 7EL
Tel: (0181) 951 5781
Fax: (0181) 951 5782

> *West Midlands Branch*
> Haydon Communications,
> Unit 1,
> Canal View Industrial Estate,
> Brettel Lane,
> BRIERLEY HILL,
> West Midlands DY5 3LO
> Tel: (01384) 481681

CM Howes Communications,
Eydon,
DAVENTRY,
Northants NN11 3PT
Tel: (01327) 260178

Javiation,
Carlton Works,
Carlton Street,
BRADFORD,
West Yorkshire BD7 1DA
Tel: (01274) 732146
Fax: (01274) 722627
Link Electronics,
216 Lincoln Road,

Millfield,
PETERBOROUGH PE1 2NE
Tel: (01733) 345731
Fax: (01733) 346770

Lowe Electronics Limited,
Chesterfield Road,
MATLOCK,
Derbyshire DE4 5LE
Tel: (01629) 580800
Fax: (01629) 580020

> *Branch Offices*
> Bristol & Wales — 79 Gloucester Road,
> Patchway, BRISTOL BS12 5QJ
> Tel: (0117) 931 5263
> Fax: (0117) 931 5270

> Northeast — Unit 18B, Airport Ind. Estate,
> NEWCASTLE UPON TYNE NE3 2EF
> Tel: (0191) 214 5424
> Fax: (0191) 214 0761

Martin Lynch & Son,
140/142 Northfield Avenue,
Ealing,
LONDON W13 9SB
Tel: (0181) 566 1120
Fax: (0181) 566 1207

Moonraker (UK) Ltd,
Unit 12,
Cranfield Road Units,
Cranfield Road,
Woburn Sands,
Bucks MK17 8UR
Tel: (01908) 281705
Fax: (01908) 281706

Multicomm,
Unit 5/7,
86 Cambridge Street,
ST NEOTS,
Cambridgeshire PE19 1PJ
Tel: (01480) 406770
Fax: (01480) 356192

Nevada Communications,
189 London Road,
North End,
PORTSMOUTH PO2 9AE
Tel: (01705) 662145
Fax: (01705) 690626

Showroom
Nevada Communications,
1A Munster Road,
PORTSMOUTH PO2 9BS

Photavia Press,
Sunrise Break,
Chiseldon Farm,
South Down Hill,
BRIXHAM,
Devon TQ5 0AE
Tel: (01803) 855599

SRP Trading,
1686 Bristol Road South,
Rednal,
BIRMINGHAM B45 9TZ
Tel: (0121) 460 1581
Fax: (0121) 457 9009

Sandpiper Communications,
Pentwyn House,
Penyard,
Llwydcoed,
ABERDARE,
Mid Glamorgan CF44 0TU
Tel: (01685) 870425

Solid State Electronics (UK),
6 The Orchard,
Bassett Green Village,
SOUTHAMPTON SO16 3NA
Tel: (01703) 769598

South Midlands Communications,
SM House,
School Close,
Chandlers Ford Industrial Estate,
EASTLEIGH,
Hants SO53 4BY
Tel: (01703) 255111
Fax: (01703) 263507

Steepletone Products Ltd,
Park End Works,
Croughton,
Brackley,
Northants NN13 5BR
Tel: (01869) 810081
Fax: (01869) 810784

Tandy Corporation
Shops in all principal towns throughout the UK
(See telephone directory for local information)

Waters & Stanton,
22 Main Road,
HOCKLEY,
Essex SS5 4QS
Tel: (01702) 206835
Fax: (01702) 205843

W. H. Westlake,
Clawton
HOLSWORTHY,
Devon EX22 6QN
Tel: (01409) 253758

Unicom,
112 Reculver Road,
Beltinge,
Herne Bay,
Kent CT6 6PD
Tel: (01227) 749352
Fax: (01227) 749352

The following organisations should be contacted
for aeronautical navigation charts for the UK
and most other areas of the world:

Westward Digital,
37 Windsor Street,
CHELTENHAM,
Glos GL52 2DG
Tel: (01242) 235151
Fax: (01242) 584139

Racal Avionics Limited,
(Aerad Charts),
Hersham House,
Lyon Road,
WALTON-ON-THAMES KT12 3PU
Tel: (0181) 946 8011
Fax: (01932) 267572

Royal Air Force,
No 1 AIDU,
RAF Northolt,
West End Road,
RUISLIP,
Middlesex HA4 6NG
Tel: (0181) 845 2300